More than just a Pot

© Naumann & Göbel Verlagsgesellschaft mbH, a subsidiary of
VEMAG Verlags- und Medien Aktiengesellschaft, Cologne
www.vemag-medien.de

Recipes: Sylvia Winnewisser
Photography: TLC Fotostudio
Translation from German: SAW Communications, Mainz,
Dr. Suzanne Kirkbright and Catherine Savile Johnson
Complete production: Naumann & Göbel Verlagsgesellschaft mbH, Cologne

ISBN: 978-3-625-11469-7

More than just a Pot

Contents

Contents

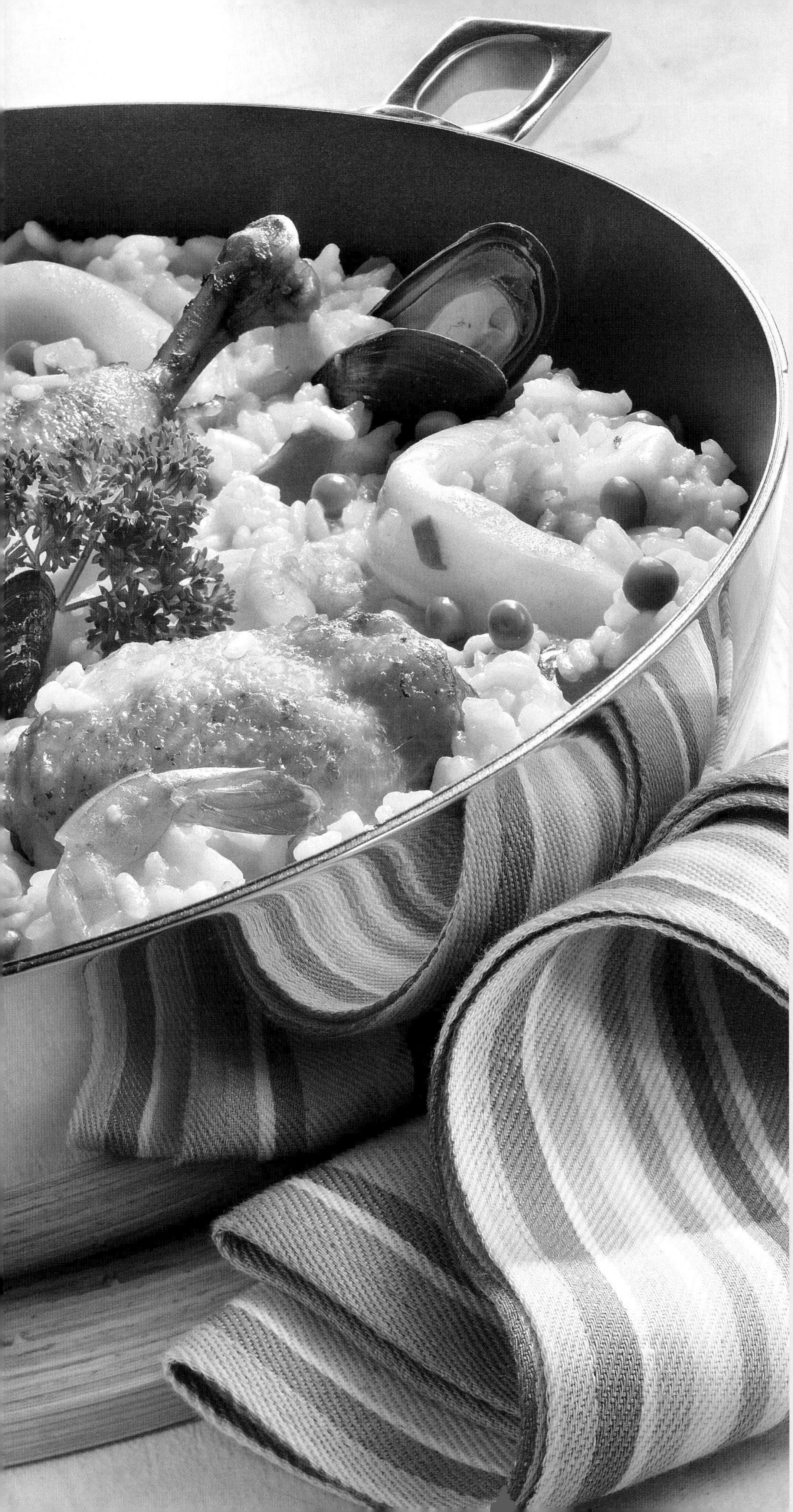

Paella Pan

Original Valencian Paella

If you have already enjoyed a vacation in Spain, or are a connoisseur of Spanish cuisine generally, then you will have heard of paella. Paella is a rice dish prepared with saffron and other ingredients. The most famous version of paella is the so-called "Paella Valenciana", the national dish of the city of Valencia in southwestern Spain. The region boasts the most fertile areas on the Spanish continent. Orchards and markets gardens bloom along the coastline, where the Mediterranean supplies fish and seafood. Paella enjoys an almost unrivalled reputation, but originally it was a dish for peasants and estate workers, who cooked in the open fields in a pan, which they filled with rice, leftovers or whatever was available. Nowadays, things are basically different. Going out for a paella ("andar de paella") is meanwhile accepted as a regular part of Valencian life. Celebrating festivals, saints, and other social occasions all revolves around the highlight of preparing this rice dish. Authentic paella consisted of rice, snails, and vegetables, such as green and white beans, bell peppers, tomatoes, and sometimes artichokes. On special occasions, pieces of chicken or rabbit were added.

Seafood paella is prepared with fresh tiger prawns, shrimp, cocktail shrimp, calamari, and mussels. There are also other variations of paella: strictly vegetarian, with sausage, black pudding, meat or seafood paella, and using pasta instead of rice. It's important for each variant of the rice-based paella to be colored yellow, by adding fresh saffron.

Traditionally, paella is mainly prepared outdoors over an open pine or almond log fire. The paella pan rests on an iron tripod, which is directly placed in the embers. They should be glowing red-hot at the start and gradually lose heat during cooking. Tradition also has it that you take the paella directly from the fire, to serve at the table, where you eat out of the pan with the (wooden) spoon.

Preparing the Paella

There are many ways to prepare paella. No single method is the right one. All paella chefs agree that the best time to consume paella is 3 pm, since it's more difficult to digest in the evening. It's also essential to add the right amount of oil for frying, as paella is not meant to taste too fatty.

The main ingredient for a successful paella is rice. Again, the consensus is that the best variety to use for paella is a special round-grain rice called "arroz bomba" and grown in the Valencia region. How you add the rice is a matter of faith: some people prefer to scatter the rice in a cross shape over the sautéed meat and vegetables, letting the rice distribute evenly; and then to add in water or stock. Others ignore the cross shape. But everybody agrees that adding more water is wrong. Incidentally, some people like to pour in a splash of beer.

Round-grain rice needs about double, or two-and-a-half times the quantity of water, so use two-and-a-half cups of water to one cup of rice. During the first ten minutes of boiling, the rice loses starch, and then it begins to absorb liquid.

Paella is not stirred. This means that the rice takes up the flavor of those ingredients cooking next to it in the pan. Stirring is avoided, so as not to spoil the taste.

Paella is ready when all the water has evaporated. The dish should be left to simmer for another few minutes so that the so-called "soccarat", the tasty fine crust, can form at the bottom of the pot when the rice begins to caramelize. Usually, a piece of newspaper is placed over the pot, to trap any rising steam.

By the way, Valencians think that Paella can only be prepared correctly using genuine Valencian water. This is why they always carry a bottle of local water with them, so if they are traveling they can cook paella whenever they like.

The Paella Pan (Paellera)

To prepare an authentic "Paella Valenciana" you need a paella pan. The real name is a "Paellera", but nowadays it is only called "paella" to match the dish you prepare in it. The original name probably comes from the Latin "patella", which basically means a "flat tablet" on which sacrifices were presented to the Gods. In 16th century Spain, a similar container was known as "paila".

The original paella pan is a large, round and flat cast-iron frying skillet with a diameter measuring 12 to 20 in/30 to 50 cm and splayed sides. The paella pan for the open fire was mostly made out of steel. Its disadvantage was that if not used regularly and seasoned afterwards with olive oil, it quickly rusted. The paella pan available from Ikea is made out of stainless steel and coated with Teflon, so it's perfectly adapted to modern lifestyles. The diameter is approximately 13 in/33 cm and the pan easily makes enough to serve 4.

The pan's wide diameter is essential if the moisture is to evaporate properly. It also helps the popular caramelized crust to form at the bottom.

The advantage of the modern paella is that it is also ovenproof. Feel free to use it for a different clay or ovenware pot besides the famous paella.

Over the next few pages, you can browse through popular paella recipes, along with other Spanish rice, fish, and vegetable dishes for you to try out in the stylish paella pan.

Bon appetit!

Peas Spanish Style

Serves 4

2 onions
4 ½ cups/900 g frozen peas
3 tbsp butter
⅔ cup/150 ml vegetable stock
½ bunch freshly chopped parsley
½ bunch freshly chopped chives
½ tsp sugar
salt, pepper
4 ½ oz/125 g Chorizo sausage
4 eggs

Preparation time: ca. 20 minutes
(plus braising and cooking time)
Per serving ca. 470 kcal/1974 kJ
31 g P, 24 g F, 32 g C

Peel and finely chop the onions. Defrost peas. Heat butter in a large skillet and sauté onions until lightly browned. Then add the peas and steam, stirring occasionally.

Pour in stock and fold in herbs and sugar. Season to taste with salt and pepper. Slice sausage and distribute around the edge of the pot. Bring mixture to a boil and simmer over low heat for about 5 minutes.

Crack the eggs one after the other into a dish and carefully let them slide over the peas, without breaking the yolks. Cover the pot if possible and fry the eggs until a film forms over the yolks. Arrange the peas in the pot. Serve with bread.

Vegetable Paella with Tuna Fish

Peel and finely chop onions and garlic. Clean and thinly slice zucchini. Clean, de-seed and remove stalks of bell peppers. Dice peppers.

Heat olive oil in a skillet and sauté garlic cloves. Deep-fry zucchini in hot oil, remove and drain on kitchen towel. Keep warm. Sauté diced pepper and onions. Remove and keep warm.

Drench tomatoes in boiling water, remove skins, stalks, and seeds and dice flesh. Place in pan and sauté, stirring occasionally. Pour in wine and season.

Return remaining vegetables to pot and bring to a boil for 5 minutes. Drain tuna fish and spread over vegetable paella. Sprinkle with basil and serve.

Serves 4

2 onions
2 garlic cloves
2 zucchini
1 red and yellow bell pepper
½ cup/125 ml olive oil
4 beef tomatoes
4 tbsp white wine
salt, pepper
14 oz/400 g canned tuna fish
2 tbsp freshly chopped basil

Preparation time: ca. 30 minutes
(plus cooking time)
Per serving ca. 623 kcal/2617 kJ
21 g P, 57 g F, 8 g C

Serves 4

1 lb 11 oz/750 g saddle of lamb fillet

2 onions

2 garlic cloves

6 tbsp olive oil

1 tsp noble sweet ground paprika

4 tbsp dry white wine

1 untreated lemon

1 tbsp freshly chopped rosemary

salt, pepper

Preparation time: ca. 20 minutes (plus braising and cooking time)
Per serving ca. 350 kcal/1470 kJ
55 g P, 12 g F, 4 g C

Lamb in Lemon Sauce

Dice lamb fillet into bite-size pieces. Peel, and finely chop onions and garlic. Heat 5 tbsp olive oil in a large paella pot and sauté diced meat on all sides. Remove meat from pot and keep warm.

Pour remaining oil into pot and heat with the lamb stock. Simmer onions, garlic, and ground paprika in stock for about 2 minutes. Return meat to pot and pour in wine. Braise the meat for about 10 minutes.

Wash the lemon in boiling water, grate zest and squeeze. Add lemon zest, juice, and rosemary to meat and season to taste with salt and pepper.

Veal Kidneys in Sherry

Peel and chop onions and garlic. Heat 4 tbsp oil in a large skillet and glaze onions with garlic and bay leaf, stirring occasionally. Fold in flour and add stock. Bring to a boil and allow to thicken. Add parsley and simmer everything for a further 3 minutes.

Clean and halve the kidneys and dice into 1 in/3 cm chunks. In a second large skillet, sauté the kidney pieces evenly in remaining hot oil for about 5 minutes. Remove from pot and keep warm.

Reduce the braising juices with the Sherry and return kidneys to pot. Add the sauce and mix well. Season and serve with saffron rice.

Serves 4

2 onions
1 garlic clove
1 bay leaf
6 tbsp olive oil
2 tbsp flour
½ cup/125 ml beef stock
2 tbsp freshly chopped parsley
1 lb 12 oz/800 g veal kidneys
salt, pepper
½ cup/125 ml dry Sherry

Preparation time: ca. 30 minutes
(plus braising and cooking time)
Per serving ca. 353 kcal/1483 kJ
33 g P, 18 g F, 9 g C

Paella from Valencia

Serves 4

1 cup/150 g frozen peas

2 tomatoes

1 red bell pepper

4 garlic cloves

2 legs of rabbit
(ca. 1 lb 2 oz/500 g)

1 roasting chicken
(ca. 2 lb 3 oz/1 kg)

9 oz/250 g calamari rings

12 blue-black mussels

6 tbsp olive oil

salt

3 ¼ cups/750 ml chicken
stock

1 tsp saffron threads

1 tbsp noble sweet ground
paprika

2 cups/400 g paella rice

14 oz/400 g unshelled,
raw tiger prawns

Preparation time: ca. 50 minutes
(plus braising and cooking time)
Per serving ca. 735 kcal/3087 kJ
82 g P, 33 g F, 26 g C

Defrost peas. Drench tomatoes in boiling water, removing skins, stalks, and seeds and dice the flesh. Clean bell pepper and cut into strips. Peel and chop garlic.

Loosen the meat from rabbit joint and dice. Cut chicken into 6 pieces, remove and cut breast fillet into chunks. Drench the calamari rings in cold water and drain. Scrub the mussels well, discarding any open shells. Allow mussels to drain in a sieve.

Heat 4 tbsp oil in a paella pan and sear strips of bell pepper. Remove from pan. Sear chicken and breast pieces in hot oil for about 10 minutes. Add garlic and rabbit and braise for a further 5 minutes. Season and remove from pot.

Pour remaining oil into pot and braise calamari rings, mussels, and tomatoes. Return meat to pot and combine well with rice. Cook paella on full heat for about 15 minutes.

Wash and pat dry the prawns and place on top of the paella. Also top with decoratively arranged strips of bell pepper. Reduce heat and simmer the paella for another 8 minutes. Remove pan from heat, cover with a newspaper and allow to simmer gently for another few minutes.

Serves 4

9 oz/250 g pork
9 oz/250 g beef
4 ½ oz/125 g ham
1 large onion
3 tbsp olive oil
generous 1 cup/220 g
long-grain rice
2 ½ cups/600 ml meat stock
2 tbsp freshly squeezed
lemon juice
4 ½ oz/125 g Chorizo
sausage
salt, pepper
3 tbsp freshly chopped
chervil

Preparation time: ca. 30 minutes
(plus braising and cooking time)
Per serving ca. 553 kcal/2323 kJ
42 g P, 23 g F, 45 g C

Hearty Rice Pan

Dice meat into 1 in/3 cm chunks, cut ham into strips. Peel and slice onion in rings.

Heat oil in a large paella pot and sear meat chunks on all sides. Add ham and onion rings and simmer for about 10 minutes, until onions are soft.

Scatter the rice around the pot and mix until well coated in the oil. Pour in stock and lemon juice. Slice the sausage and place in pot.

Bring the ingredients to a boil and simmer over low heat for about 25 minutes, until the rice is done. Season and serve with a sprinkling of chervil.

Serves 4

1 small cauliflower
3 tomatoes
2 garlic cloves
4 artichokes
1 cup/200 g frozen peas
½ lemon, juiced
1 quart/1 l vegetable stock
4 tbsp olive oil
1 tsp hot paprika
2 cups/400 g paella rice
1 small can saffron threads
salt

Preparation time: ca. 30 minutes
(plus braising and cooking time)
Per serving ca. 313 kcal/1315 kJ
19 g P, 15 g F, 26 g C

Vegetable Paella

Clean cauliflower and break into small florets. Drench tomatoes with boiling water. Remove skins, stalks, and seeds and dice flesh. Peel and chop garlic.

Cut off artichoke stems at the base, discarding the outer leaves. Cut off tops of leaves and quarter the artichokes, removing straw. Drizzle with lemon juice. Defrost peas.

Heat oil in a paella pan and sauté garlic, cauliflower, and tomatoes. Season with paprika. Heat and pour in stock. Bring to a boil, stir in the rice and simmer for 3 minutes.

Add artichokes and peas and season with saffron and salt. Cook all ingredients for about 10 minutes, then reduce heat and simmer for a further 10 minutes.

Chicken with Saffron Rice

Serves 4

1 spring chicken,
ca. 3 lb 1 oz/1 ½ kg

salt, pepper

1 tbsp clarified butter

4 ½ oz/125 g smoked
bacon

2 onions

1 garlic clove

1 tbsp hot ground paprika

3 tomatoes

1 ¾ cups/350 g rice

1 ½ cups/300 g peas

3 ¼ cups/750 ml chicken
stock

⅛ tsp ground saffron

2 tbsp flat leaf parsley,
freshly chopped

Preparation time: ca. 30 minutes
(plus braising and cooking time)
Per serving ca. 673 kcal/2827 kJ
47 g P, 18 g F, 80 g C

Divide the chicken into 6–8 portions and season with salt and pepper. Heat clarified butter in a large paella pan. Dice the bacon, peel and chop onions and garlic. Sauté diced bacon in the pot until crispy. Remove and leave to drain on kitchen towel. Place chicken portions in the pot and sear on all sides. Remove from heat and keep warm.

Drain off the surplus fat. Glaze onions and garlic in remaining fat for 5 minutes, stir in paprika. Meanwhile, drench tomatoes in boiling water, skin, remove stalks, de-seed and dice the flesh. Place diced tomato in pot and steam off the liquid.

Add chicken, bacon, rice, peas, stock, and saffron and combine well. Simmer over a medium heat for about 25 minutes, until the rice is done and chicken tender. Season with salt and pepper, stir in parsley. Remove pot from heat, cover and let settle for a few minutes.

Rice with Mussels

Wash and scrub the mussels, discarding any open shells. Peel and chop garlic. Wash and dice the bell pepper. Wash, shake dry and chop the parsley, reserving a few whole sprigs.

Heat oil in a pot and glaze garlic with the diced pepper. Stir in and lightly sauté the rice. Pour in stock and bring to a boil. Simmer over low heat for 15 minutes until the rice is done.

Boil mussels in a large pan in generous 1 cup/250 ml salty water for 5 minutes. Occasionally shake the pot. When the shells open, pour off the liquid and leave mussels to drain, reserving the braising juices. Loosen flesh from the mussel shells. Discard any unopened mussels.

Stir mussels and parsley into the rice and pour in reserved cooking juices. Simmer for another 8 minutes. Remove the pan from the heat, cover and allow to rest for 5 minutes. Garnish with parsley sprigs and serve.

Serves 4

4 lb 7 oz/2 kg clams
2 garlic cloves
1 red bell pepper
1 bunch flat leaf parsley
4 tbsp olive oil
2 cups/400 g paella rice
3 ⅓ cups/800 ml vegetable stock

Preparation time: ca. 30 minutes
(plus braising and cooking time)
Per serving ca. 640 kcal/2688 kJ
35 g P, 13 g F, 94 g C

21

Seafood Paella

Defrost peas. Loosen the chicken from the bone and dice. Wash seafood and cut into small pieces. Shell prawns, removing the intestine. Scrub the mussels thoroughly, discarding any open shells. Clean and dice the bell pepper. Peel and chop onion and garlic.

Heat 4 tbsp olive oil in a paella pan and sauté onions with the garlic and diced pepper. Remove from pot. Add chicken and sear on all sides, then also remove from the pot and keep warm.

Heat remaining oil in the pot and sauté the seafood, turning occasionally. Stir in the rice, so that it is well coated in oil. Add stock and return the reserved warm ingredients to the pot. Season with saffron and allspice.

Cook the paella for about 20 minutes at full heat, then reduce the temperature and allow everything to braise for a further 8 minutes. Season to taste with salt and pepper.

Serves 4

¾ cup/150 g frozen peas
generous 1 lb/500 g chicken
1 lb/450 g mixed seafood (e.g. mussels, baby squid, crab, and lobster flesh, prawns)
1 red bell pepper
1 onion
2 garlic cloves
6 tbsp olive oil
1 ¾ cups/350 g paella rice
3 ¼ cups/750 ml chicken stock
1 bag saffron threads
½ tsp ground allspice
salt, pepper

Preparation time: ca. 30 minutes (plus braising and cooking time)
Per serving ca. 605 kcal/2541 kJ
54 g P, 8 g F, 78 g C

Sauté Potatoes Spanish Style

Serves 4

18 small potatoes
3 tbsp butter
4 tbsp olive oil
½ bunch coriander
salt, pepper
1 tsp noble sweet ground paprika

Preparation time: ca. 20 minutes
(plus cooking and frying time)
Per serving ca. 213 kcal/895 kJ
3 g P, 12 g F, 23 g C

Boil potatoes in salted water for about 30 minutes. Drain and allow to cool slightly. Peel and halve potatoes.

Heat the butter and olive oil in a large pan and sauté the potatoes, turning several times until golden brown all over.

Wash, pat dry and finely chop the coriander. Add to the potatoes and combine well. Season potatoes with salt and pepper and sauté for another 1–2 minutes. Serve coriander potatoes with meat dishes.

Spanish Omelet (Tortilla) with Onions

Peel and thinly slice the potatoes. Peel and chop onions. Heat ½ cup/ 125 ml oil in a large paella pan.

Add potato slices, season with salt and coat in oil by tossing several times. Sauté over low heat for approximately 10 minutes. Add onions and cook for another 10 minutes. Allow the potato mixture to drain in a sieve.

Whisk the eggs with ½ tsp salt and combine with the potato mixture. Heat remaining olive oil in the pot and add the omelet mixture. Distribute evenly around the pot and allow to thicken over low heat for about 3 minutes.

Cover the pot with a large plate, upturn and turn the omelet out onto the plate. Carefully slide the omelet back into the pot and sauté on the other side.

Serves 4

2 ¼ lb/1 kg potatoes
3 small onions
⅔ cup/160 ml olive oil
2 tsp salt
6 eggs

Preparation time: ca. 30 minutes
(plus cooking and frying time)
Per serving ca. 550 kcal/2310 kJ
17 g P, 35 g F, 40 g C

Braised Spinach

Serves 4

6 tbsp sultanas

2 small onions

1 garlic clove

3 ½ oz/100 g Serrano ham

2 ¼ lb/1 kg fresh spinach

3 tbsp olive oil

⅓ cup/50 g roasted pine nuts

salt, pepper

½ tsp ground nutmeg

Preparation time: ca. 20 minutes
(plus braising and cooking time)
Per serving ca. 231 kcal/970 kJ
15 g P, 12 g F, 14 g C

Soak the sultanas in boiling water and leave for approximately 30 minutes. Pour away the liquid and let drain. Peel and chop onions and garlic. Slice the ham into thin strips.

Sort and clean the spinach, removing and roughly chopping the hard stems. Heat the oil in the paella pan. Glaze onions and garlic in the pot. Add strips of ham and sauté everything for 5 minutes until the onions are soft.

Add the spinach to the pot and steam, stirring until the spinach reduces. Stir in pine nuts and sultanas, heat and season the spinach with salt, pepper, and nutmeg.

Braised Cauliflower

Clean and break the cauliflower into florets. Drizzle with lemon juice in a bowl. Peel and chop garlic.

Heat olive oil in the paella pan and fry the sliced bread on both sides until crispy. Then, dice into small chunks and purée with garlic, sunflower seeds, and parsley.

Add the ground paprika to the pot and lightly roast for 2 minutes in the oil. Pour in stock and bring to a boil. Braise the cauliflower in the stock for 12 minutes, until cooked.

Mix some of the cauliflower juice with the puréed ingredients and add to the pot. Cook everything for a further 5 minutes, then season to taste with salt and pepper.

Serves 4

2 ¼ lb/1 kg cauliflower
2 tsp lemon juice
3 garlic cloves
⅓ cup/80 ml olive oil
3 slices white bread
2 tbsp roasted sunflower seeds
3 tbsp freshly chopped flat leaf parsley
1 tbsp hot ground paprika
2 cups/500 ml vegetable stock
salt, pepper

Preparation time: ca. 20 minutes
(plus braising and cooking time)
Per serving ca. 258 kcal/1084 kJ
9 g P, 16 g F, 19 g C

27

Paella with Snails

Serves 6

1 ¼ cups/250 g dried white beans
1 chicken, ca. 2 lb 10 oz/1 ¼ kg
salt, pepper
2 onions
2 garlic cloves
4 tomatoes
1 ¼ quarts/1 ¼ l chicken stock
24 snails, canned
9 oz/250 g green beans
½ tsp saffron threads
2 cups/400 g paella rice
2 lemons

Preparation time: ca. 40 minutes (plus marinating, braising and cooking time)
Per serving ca. 603 kcal/2533 kJ
42 g P, 11 g F, 80 g C

Soak the beans overnight in water. Cook in boiling water for about 60 minutes, pour off the liquid and allow to drain. Cut the chicken into several portions and season with salt and pepper.

Peel and dice onions and garlic. Drench tomatoes in boiling water, remove skins and stalks, de-seed and dice. Heat oil in the pot and sear the chicken portions all over for about 7 minutes. Remove from pot and set aside.

Place onions, garlic, and tomatoes in the pot and simmer for about 10 minutes, stirring occasionally. Return chicken to the pot. Pour in stock and bring to a boil.

Drain the snails. Clean the green beans and cut into small pieces, as desired. Add the snails, two bean varieties, and rice to the pot and mix well. Fold in the saffron. Cook the paella for about 20 minutes, until the rice has absorbed the liquid.

When cooked, remove the pot from the heat, cover (preferably with newspaper) and let settle for 5 to 10 minutes. Serve in the pot and garnish with lemon eighths.

Serves 4

12 small potatoes

1 onion

1 bay leaf

1 lb 11 oz/750 g hake fillet

5 tbsp olive oil

4 garlic cloves

1 can chopped tomatoes
(generous 2 cups/400 g)

salt, pepper

1 tbsp noble sweet ground
paprika

2 tbsp freshly chopped dill

Preparation time: ca. 30 minutes
(plus cooking and braising time)
Per serving ca. 358 kcal/1504 kJ
37 g P, 11 g F, 26 g C

Hake with Vegetable Sauce

Peel and halve the potatoes. Peel onions and cut into rings. Bring 2 quarts/2 l water to a boil in the paella pan. Add potatoes, onions, and bay leaf and simmer everything for about 20 minutes, until the potatoes are cooked. Remove potatoes from the pan. Add the fish fillets to the pot and allow to simmer in the liquid over low heat for 7 minutes. When the fish breaks up, it is done.

Heat oil in a second pot. Peel and halve the garlic and sauté in the hot oil. Remove from pot. Place tomatoes in the pan with a little salt and simmer until they form a thick paste. Season with paprika.

Drain away the fish stock, reserving 1 cup/250 ml, and remove onion rings and bay leaf. Add the potatoes to the fish. Top with the tomato paste. Simmer everything for another 5 minutes, coating the fish and potatoes well with the sauce. Sprinkle with dill and serve.

Serves 4

generous 1 lb/500 g cured
cod (stockfish)
1 lb 11 oz/750 g potatoes
8 tbsp olive oil
2 onions
2 garlic cloves
2 tbsp freshly chopped flat
leaf parsley
salt, pepper
black olives for garnish

Preparation time: ca. 30 minutes
(plus cooking, braising
and baking time)
Per serving ca. 693 kcal/2911 kJ
99 g P, 18 g F, 31 g C

Cured Cod Gratin

Drench the cured cod thoroughly with water, drain and place in a pot. Cover with water and cook for about 15 minutes. Divide fish into pieces, de-bone and skin. Peel potatoes and cook for about 20 minutes in boiling salted water. Drain and slice.

Heat 2 tbsp oil in the paella pan. Peel onions and cut into rings. Peel and chop garlic. Sauté onions and garlic in the oil for approximately 6 minutes until glassy. Then remove from pot.

Heat 3 tbsp oil in the pot and sauté sliced potato on each side, then remove. Preheat oven to 390 °F/200 °C. Grease the pot with 1 tbsp oil. Fill alternately with potatoes, cured cod, and onions. Season with salt and pepper.

Drizzle the gratin with remaining oil and bake in the oven for about 25 minutes. Serve garnished with olives.

Paella au Gratin

Serves 4

½ cup/100 g chickpeas

2 garlic cloves

2 onions

1 bay leaf

1 ½ quarts/1 ½ l vegetable stock

1 chicken, ca. 2 lb 10 oz/ 1 ¼ kg

3 ½ oz/100 g cooked ham

5 oz/150 g black pudding

3 tbsp olive oil

2 cups/400 g paella rice

salt, pepper

½ tsp noble sweet ground paprika

½ tsp cumin

½ tsp saffron threads

2 eggs

2 tbsp breadcrumbs

Preparation time: ca. 30 minutes (plus cooking, braising and baking time)
Per serving ca. 915 kcal/3843 kJ
55 g P, 38 g F, 89 g C

Soak the chickpeas overnight. Peel and chop garlic and onions. Cut the chicken into eight portions and slice black pudding. Dice the ham.

Bring chickpeas to a boil in the stock with garlic, onions, and bay leaf. Add the chicken and black pudding and cook for approximately 45 minutes. Remove bay leaf. Drain chickpeas and reserve stock.

Preheat the oven to 440 °F/225 °C. Heat olive oil in the paella pan. Add the diced ham and rice and simmer, stirring occasionally, until the rice is coated in oil. Add another 1 quart/1 l stock and stir in spices. Simmer for 10 minutes.

Mix black pudding and chicken into the rice and simmer everything for another 5 minutes. Whisk the eggs and pour over the mixture. Sprinkle breadcrumbs over the dish and bake in the oven for about 20 minutes until golden yellow.

Serves 4

4 ½ lb/2 kg filleted, mixed fish
salt, pepper
2 lemons, juiced
1 onion
1 bay leaf
2 cloves
3 tbsp olive oil
2 garlic cloves
2 cups/400 g paella rice
½ tsp saffron threads
1 tsp noble sweet ground paprika
½ tsp turmeric
2 tbsp freshly chopped coriander

Rice Pan with Fish

Preparation time: ca. 30 minutes
(plus cooking and braising time)
Per serving ca. 615 kcal/2583 kJ
53 g P, 8 g F, 80 g C

Clean, dry and cut the fish into several portions. Season with salt and pepper. Drizzle immediately with lemon juice. Set aside.

Peel and spike the onion with bay leaf and cloves. Bring 1 quart/1 l water to a boil in a pot and add the onion. Add the fish portions and cook over a medium heat for about 15 minutes. Lift out the fish and keep warm.

Heat oil in the paella pan. Peel and chop garlic. Sauté garlic and rice in the hot oil, until the rice is glassy. Pour in 1 quart/1 l fish stock and stir in the spices. Cook rice for approximately 20 minutes. When the liquid is absorbed, stir in fish pieces and warm in the rice. Serve with a sprinkling of coriander.

Black Squid Paella

Carefully remove the ink sac from the squid and cook in boiling salted water for about 10 minutes.

Peel and finely chop garlic. Clean and cut the bell pepper into fine strips. Clean, de-seed and slice the chili into thin rings. Drench tomatoes in boiling water, remove the skins, stalks, de-seed and dice.

Heat oil in the paella pan. Sauté strips of bell pepper and chili with the garlic. Add tomatoes, stir in lemon juice and gently cook everything for around 10 minutes, until the liquid has evaporated. Purée the mixture.

Lightly sauté rice in the remaining oil. Add vegetable purée and pour in stock. Cook the rice for about 20 minutes.

Whilst the rice is cooking, open the ink sac and mix the ink and wine. Drain rice in a sieve. Stir in small pieces of squid and season everything with salt and pepper. Cook the squid and rice for about 20 minutes and serve with garlic mayonnaise.

Serves 4

2 lb 3 oz/1 kg prepared baby squid with ink sac
salt
1 garlic clove
1 green bell pepper
1 red chili
2 tomatoes
5 tbsp olive oil
1 lemon, juiced
3 ¼ cups/750 ml vegetable stock
2 tbsp freshly chopped flat leaf parsley
2 cups/400 g paella rice
½ cup/125 ml dry white wine
pepper

Preparation time: ca. 40 minutes (plus braising and cooking time)
Per serving ca. 590 kcal/2478 kJ
48 g P, 3 g F, 86 g C

Paella with Pasta

Serves 4

2 onions

2 garlic cloves

3 tomatoes

4 tbsp olive oil

3 ⅓ cups/800 ml fish stock

14 oz/400 g monkfish

salt, pepper

1 tsp noble sweet ground paprika

1 tbsp freshly chopped parsley

14 oz/400 g short Spanish pasta ("fideos")

3 ½ oz/100 g peeled, raw prawns

Preparation time: ca. 40 minutes (plus braising, cooking and baking time)
Per serving ca. 518 kcal/2176 kJ
34 g P, 10 g F, 72 g C

Peel and chop onions and garlic. Drench tomatoes in boiling water, remove the skins and stalks, de-seed and dice.

Heat 2 tbsp oil in a paella pan and sauté onions and garlic. Add diced tomatoes and pour in fish stock. Bring to a boil and add the pre-diced fish fillets. Season with spices and stir in parsley.

Add pasta to the pot and simmer the paella until the liquid has almost evaporated. Preheat the oven to 350 °F/175 °C.

Heat the remaining oil in a second pot and sauté prawns until they turn pink. Add to the paella and bake in the oven for about 7 minutes. Serve in the pot.

Paella with Mushrooms and Chorizo

Clean, de-seed and cut the bell pepper into strips. Loosen the chicken from the bone and dice. Slice the Chorizo. Dampen, clean off and slice the mushrooms. Peel and chop garlic. Drench tomatoes in boiling water, remove the skins and stalks, de-seed and dice flesh. Clean beans and cut into small chunks.

Heat the oil in a paella pan and sauté the bell pepper for 5 minutes, then remove. Sear the chicken for 10 minutes, turning occasionally. Remove the meat and sauté the sliced sausage. Remove sausage and sauté mushrooms, garlic, and lemon zest in the pan.

Add tomatoes to the pot and simmer everything for a further 5 minutes. Add beans, herbs, saffron, rice, chicken, and sausage and pour in stock. Without covering, simmer gently over low heat for approximately 30 minutes. Remove pot from heat and season the paella to taste with salt and pepper. Cover with a newspaper and leave to settle for another 10 minutes. Garnish with lemon eighths and serve.

Serves 4

1 red bell pepper
1 lb 5 oz/600 g chicken
5 oz/150 g Chorizo sausage
5 oz/150 g mushrooms
3 garlic cloves
generous 1 lb/500 g tomatoes
5 oz/150 g green beans
¼ cup/60 ml olive oil
1 tbsp untreated grated lemon zest
1 tbsp freshly chopped thyme and rosemary
2 tbsp freshly chopped parsley
½ tsp ground saffron
2 cups/400 g paella rice
3 ¼ cups/750 ml chicken stock
salt, pepper
2 untreated lemons, cut into eight pieces

Preparation time: ca. 30 minutes
(plus braising and cooking time)
Per serving ca. 770 kcal/3234 kJ
54 g P, 21 g F, 88 g C

Serves 4

1 prepared rabbit
(ca. 3 lb 1 oz/1 ½ kg)

salt, pepper

3 shallots

1 garlic clove

2 red and 2 yellow bell peppers

5 tbsp olive oil

2 tbsp fresh tarragon

1 tsp fennel seeds

½ cup/125 ml Vermouth

1 cup/250 ml poultry stock

Preparation time: ca. 30 minutes
(plus braising time)
Per serving ca. 463 kcal/1945 kJ
51 g P, 25 g F, 7 g C

Braised Rabbit

Cut rabbit into 6–8 portions, or pre-order the meat already prepared from your butcher. Peel shallots and cut into slivers. Peel and chop garlic. Clean bell pepper and cut lengthwise in strips.

Preheat the oven to 355 °F/180 °C. Heat the oil in a large pan and sear the rabbit pieces all over. Add garlic and shallots and simmer.

Stir in tarragon and fennel and simmer with the other ingredients for 2 minutes. Pour in the Vermouth and ½ cup/125 ml stock, bring to a boil, then add bell pepper strips and season with salt and pepper. Bake everything for about 40 minutes in the oven.

Halfway through, turn the rabbit portions and pour in remaining stock. Finally, season and serve with pasta.

Braised Swordfish

Slice and season the swordfish with salt. Leave to marinade for about 10 minutes. Toss fish steaks in flour and shake off any surplus flour. Peel and chop garlic and shallots. Clean mussels, scrubbing thoroughly and discarding any opened shells. Defrost peas. Drain the asparagus.

Heat oil in a large pot and sauté shallots with the garlic until they are glassy. Add fish pieces and sear all over. Pour in white wine. Add mussels and peas and allow to simmer for 10 minutes, frequently shaking the pot. Finally, stir in and warm the asparagus in the mixture.

Season the fish steaks to taste with spices. Remove any unopened mussels before serving. Braised swordfish goes well with a side order of fresh bread.

Serves 4

1 ¾ lb/800 g swordfish
salt
⅔ cup/100 g flour
4 garlic cloves
2 shallots
9 oz/250 g clams
1 ⅓ cups/200 g frozen peas
7 oz/200 g asparagus spears, from the jar
5 tbsp olive oil
½ cup/125 ml dry white wine
pepper
½ tsp noble sweet ground paprika

Preparation time: ca. 20 minutes (plus braising time)
Per serving ca. 495 kcal/2079 kJ
54 g P, 15 g F, 30 g C

Paella with Chicken

Serves 4

1 roasting chicken,
ca. 2 lb 10 oz/1 ¼ kg

2 onions

1 garlic clove

2 zucchini

9 oz/250 g button
mushrooms

10 ½ oz/300 g cauliflower

4 tomatoes

6 tbsp olive oil

salt, pepper

1 bunch freshly chopped
parsley

10 ½ oz/300 g broad beans,
canned

2 cups/500 ml vegetable
stock

1 tbsp saffron

1 cup/150 g frozen peas

1 ½ cups/300 g paella rice

1 ¾ oz/50 g pitted black
olives

Preparation time: a. 30 minutes
(plus braising time)
Per serving ca. 715 kcal/3003 kJ
46 g P, 26 g F, 74 g C

Divide the chicken into 8 portions. Peel and slice onions and garlic. Clean zucchini, dampen and clean off button mushrooms and slice both ingredients. Clean cauliflower and divide into florets. Drench tomatoes in boiling water, remove the skins and stalks, de-seed and dice.

Heat the oil in a large pot and sear chicken portions all over. Remove from pot and sauté onions with the garlic. Add zucchini and cauliflower and simmer. Then add mushrooms and parsley and allow to simmer for another 5 minutes.

Add diced tomato with broad beans and the liquid to the pot. Pour in stock and bring everything to a boil. Stir in saffron. Simmer the mixture over a medium heat for about 10 minutes. Add cauliflower, chicken, defrosted peas, and rice and continue to simmer for 20 minutes. Finally, top the paella with a scattering of olives, cover and let settle for about 10 minutes.

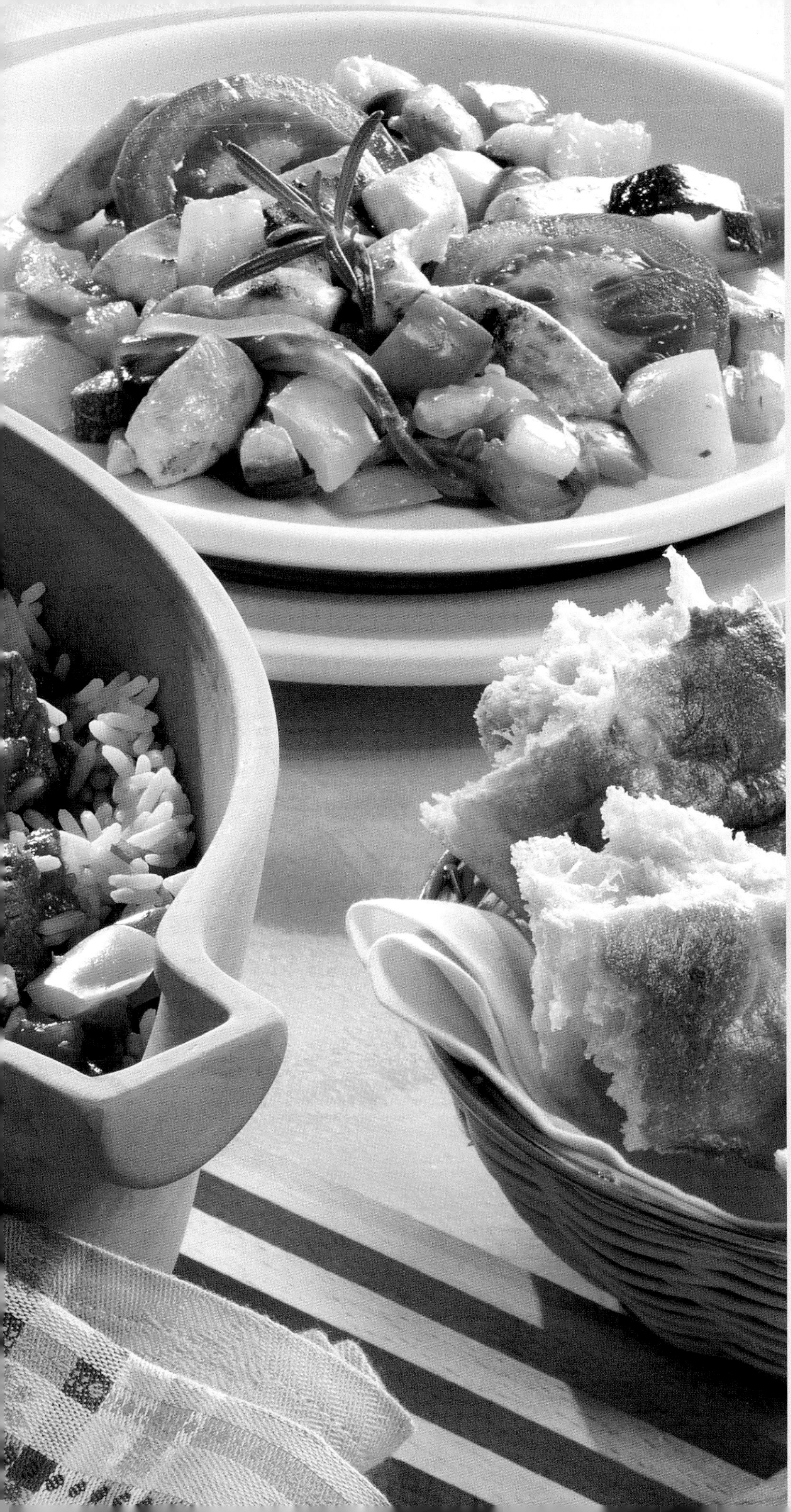

Clay Pot

The Old, New Art of Cooking in Clay Pots

Cooking in clay pots is one of the oldest methods of food preparation. Ingredients cook in the clay pot with a minimum of extra liquid, as the steaming process is more or less redundant. This process preserves taste, nutrients and vitamins, which are not drained away with the surplus cooking liquid. The clay pot means that food can be cooked gently, without adding extra fat – an ideal preparation for diabetics or patients with stomach or liver complaints. Using a clay pot is simple: the whole pot is immersed in water, so that the clay absorbs all the liquid. Cooking occurs at relatively low temperatures; the moistened clay ensures an even distribution of vapors inside the pot, thus preventing the ingredients from drying out.

The clay pot is a real cooking virtuoso that can almost do it all – from cooking to frying and baking. In a clay pot, sweets can be prepared just as easily as savories, tender poultry just the same as rustic lamb, and delicate vegetables as well as strong cabbage. The unique flavor of the vegetables and the meat derives from the perfect cooking method and also wonderfully combines with aromas from other ingredients. Everything happens in one pot almost of its own accord, so it is extremely easy to cook in the clay pot. Once the pot is in the oven, you can relax and look forward to an enjoyable meal. Food cannot burn or boil over and a few more minutes in the oven will not spoil the meal.

The Proper Usage

You will enjoy years of pleasure from your prized clay pot, providing that you treat this delicate kitchen utensil with care. The most important point is to soak the pot in cold water every time you use it. The easiest way to do this is in the kitchen drainer or in a small plastic basin. The pot has to be totally immersed in water for about 20 minutes (and for at least 30 minutes the first time you use it).

Clay pots are not resistant to large temperature swings, as they may crack. If ingredients are precooked or fried, they first have to be left to cool down to room temperature, before transferring to a cold pot. Liquids also have to be poured in cold before cooking. During cooking it's the reverse: only put hot ingredients into the hot clay pot!

The clay pot is always placed in a cold oven. Only then do you turn up the heat to the required temperature for electric ovens – and that's all. To protect the pot, first turn the heat gauge to half the required cooking temperature and increase the heat after five minutes, until after approximately 10–15 minutes, the right temperature is reached.

The clay pot is best stored in a dry and airy place. The pot does not like musty, damp basements, not to mention plastic packaging or bags, where it might even start to go moldy.

The Proper Care

Set to work immediately after cooking: you need to clean your clay pot with hot, clear water and a scrubbing brush. You can use a few drops of detergent, but definitely no abrasive liquid. This sinks into the clay pores, leaving an unpleasant taste for the next time. You can clean the pot with watered-down vinegar to remove any aromas and then re-immerse the dish in hot water. Dry with a dishcloth, kitchen towel or set on a wire cooling rack and allow drying out completely.

Tips and Tricks

Take care! The lid is just as hot as the base. Only handle the pot with an ovenproof cloth and leave on an ovenproof surface, such as a wooden board or thick towel, where it does not cool down too quickly. Take care never to add hot ingredients to the cold pot. Conversely, before adding any extra liquid to the hot dish, it must be preheated. Season your clay pot slowly, i. e. at the beginning, do not cook any dishes with very strong aromas (garlic, herbs). Potent odors may be difficult to neutralize afterwards when the pot is immersed in water. If you cook frequently in the clay pot, you may consider obtaining a second one for mild or sweet dishes and one for spicy food. Only check to see if extra liquid should be added if you are cooking tender meat or over long cooking periods. Streaky meat does not dry out so quickly; and over a short cooking time, the amount of water inside the pot is usually sufficient. Even if you take good care of the clay pot, it will turn a darker color. However, this does not change its excellent cooking qualities; discoloring is a normal process caused by the natural material.

Green Pilau

Serves 4

1 ½ cups/300 g basmati rice

2 cups/500 ml vegetable stock

2 cups/500 ml mushroom stock

14 oz/400 g broccoli

14 oz/400 g Romanesco (broccoli)

3 garlic cloves

4 tbsp olive oil

6 tbsp pine nuts

9 oz/250 g peeled tomatoes

salt, pepper

1 bunch lemon grass

Preparation time: ca. 25 minutes (plus cooking time)
Per serving ca. 345 kcal/1449 kJ
12 g P, 4 g F, 62 g C

Place the rice in a sieve and soak under running water. Add to a pre-moistened clay pot with vegetable and mushroom stock, close the lid and cook for approximately 30 minutes at 390 °F/200 °C.

Clean and wash the broccoli and Romanesco and divide into florets. Peel and finely chop the garlic.

Heat the oil in a skillet. Sauté the garlic, pine nuts, and tomatoes gently for 3–4 minutes. Season to create a spicy taste with pepper and salt.

At the end of the cooking time, stir in vegetable and garlic mixture with rice and cook for a further 30 minutes in the sealed pot.

Wash, dry and finely chop lemon grass. Remove pilau rice from oven and stir in lemon grass. Arrange on plates and serve.

Caribbean Duck Stew

Mix spices with garlic oil. Wash, pat dry and cut duck breast into thin strips. Add duck strips to garlic marinade and leave to soak for 30 minutes.

Peel shallots, carrots, and parsnips, washing and dicing them into approximately ¾ in/2 cm chunks. Clean, wash, de-seed and dice bell peppers. Loosen maize from cobs.

Place marinade and duck in a pan and sear for about 4–5 minutes, while stirring. Then add vegetables and simmer for a further 2–3 minutes.

Wash rice and add to the pre-moistened clay pot. Add vegetable mixture and stock and cover with tomato purée. Close the lid and bake everything in the oven for about 40–50 minutes at 390 °F/ 200 °C. Peel and slice bananas, arranging them on soup bowls or plates. Stir stew, pouring over bananas and serve immediately.

Serves 4

2 tbsp mild paprika
1 tbsp hot paprika
2 tbsp chili powder
1–2 tbsp cumin
½ tbsp cayenne pepper
2 tbsp garlic salt
2 tbsp garlic powder
1 tsp madras curry powder
1 tsp turmeric
2 tbsp crushed oregano
2 tbsp crushed thyme
7 tbsp garlic oil
generous 1 lb/500 g
duck breast
(skinned and off bone)
4 shallots
4 carrots
4 wild parsnips
2 red bell peppers
2 green bell peppers
6 fresh maize cobs
1 cup/200 g risotto rice
(e. g. Arborio)
1 ½ quarts/1 ½ l poultry
stock
6–8 tbsp tomato purée
4 bananas

Preparation time: ca. 25 minutes
(plus marinating and
cooking time)
Per serving ca. 1102 kcal/4628 kJ
55 g P, 44 g F, 117 g C

Serves 4

2 cups/400 g red lentils

12 small onions

2 garlic cloves

1 mild red chili

1 medium zucchini

10 ½ oz/300 g boiled
potatoes

1 pack tomato purée

2 ½ cups/600 ml vegetable
stock

1 rosemary sprig

salt

freshly milled pepper

Preparation time: ca. 20 minutes
(plus cooking time)
Per serving ca. 217 kcal/910 kJ
12 g P, 1 g F, 37 g C

Oriental Lentil Stew

Wash and allow lentils to drain. Peel onions, leaving them whole. Peel and slice garlic. Clean chilies, wash, de-seed and cut into rings. Clean, wash and slice the zucchini. Peel and dice cooled potatoes.

Place lentils in the base of a well-moistened clay pot. Top with a layer of onions, garlic and remaining vegetables. Add puréed tomatoes and vegetable stock and lightly stir.

Wash, dry and add rosemary. Season with salt and pepper, close lid and cook in the oven at 390 °F/200 °C for about 60 minutes. Serve with fresh white bread on the side.

Thai Zucchini

Wash zucchini and halve lengthways, cut off stalk and hollow out insides. Set aside.

Clean, wash and roughly chop chilies. Wash and shake dry coriander leaves.

Purée zucchini with chili, coriander, coconut flakes, lemon juice, soy sauce, and Sherry. Season with lemon pepper to create a tangy taste.

Spread mixture into zucchini halves and place in a pre-moistened clay pot. Pour in Asia stock and coat vegetables with sesame oil.

Close lid and bake at 390 °F/200 °C for approximately 45 minutes. Arrange prepared zucchini halves on preheated plates and serve. Rice makes a tasty side order.

Serves 4

4 zucchini (à ca. 7–8 ½ oz/ 200–250 g)
2 red and 2 green chilies
2 bunches coriander leaves
12 oz/350 g coconut flakes
4–6 tbsp lemon juice
4–6 tbsp soy sauce
2–3 tbsp dry Sherry
lemon pepper
1 ½ cups/350 ml instant Asia stock
6 tbsp seasoned sesame oil

Preparation time: ca. 25 minutes (plus cooking time)
Per serving ca. 575 kcal/2415 kJ
8 g P, 57 g F, 9 g C

Quinoa Ragout

Serves 4

2 ¼ lb/1 kg eggplant
salt
4 shallots
2 garlic cloves
4 tbsp olive oil
14 oz/400 g quinoa
½ cup–1 cup/⅛– ¼ l vegetable stock
1–2 tbsp lemon juice
2–3 tsp each of paprika, cayenne pepper, ground cloves, freshly ground nutmeg
3 tbsp freshly chopped basil
½ tbsp chopped rosemary leaves

Preparation time: ca. 30 minutes (plus cooking time)
Per serving ca. 77 kcal/323 kJ
3 g P, 2 g F, 8 g C

Wash eggplant, removing stems and cut into ½–⅔ in/ 1–1 ½ cm thick slices. Sprinkle slices with salt, place in a sieve and allow to drain for approximately 15–20 minutes.

Peel and finely chop shallots and garlic and sauté in oil for approximately 3–4 minutes.

Place quinoa in a pre-moistened clay pot. Mix vegetable stock with shallot-onion mass, lemon juice, and paprika. Bake for 45 minutes at 390 °F/200 °C.

Thoroughly soak eggplant, press out flesh and dice. Halfway through cooking, add spices and herbs to quinoa and mix in well. Serve in the pot.

53

Serves 4

2 large onions

1 garlic clove

5 tbsp goose fat

2 tbsp noble sweet paprika

2 tbsp hot ground paprika

1 ¾ lb/800 g chicken goulash

4 green bell peppers

14 oz/400 g peeled tomatoes

scant 2 cups/450 ml chicken stock

salt, pepper

1–2 tbsp crushed marjoram

½ tbsp whole caraway seeds

9 oz/250 g refrigerated Spätzle (German egg noodles)

chopped parsley for garnish

Chicken Goulash with German Spätzle

Preparation time: ca. 15 minutes (plus cooking time)
Per serving ca. 595 kcal/2499 kJ
53 g P, 19 g F, 51 g C

Peel and slice onions and garlic. Sauté in hot goose fat for 3–4 minutes. Stir in paprika and lightly roast for approximately 3–4 minutes. Add meat and sear for 4–5 minutes. Place everything in a pre-moistened clay pot.

Clean bell peppers, wash and chop into small pieces. Add to goulash, along with tomatoes, stock and seasoning. Bake in oven with the lid closed for about 55–65 minutes at 390 °F/200 °C.

Prepare the Spätzle according to instructions on the packet. Pass through a sieve and allow to drain. Arrange German Spätzle and goulash and serve immediately with a sprinkling of parsley.

Serves 4

8 prepared spring chicken
salt, pepper
3 crushed bay leaves
1–2 tbsp orange flavoring,
from zest
4 tbsp lime juice
10 ½ oz/300 g fresh dates
1 ¾ cups/250 g pine nuts
7 oz/200 g bitter orange
English marmalade
1 tsp each of caraway,
allspice, cardamom, and
ginger powder
10 ½ oz/300 g each
kumquats and physalis
5 tbsp clarified butter
8–10 sage leaves
2 cups/500 ml chicken stock
6 tbsp natural yogurt

Oriental Spring Chicken

Preparation time: ca. 20 minutes
(plus cooking time)
Per serving ca. 1293 kcal/5429 kJ
55 g P, 72 g F, 106 g C

Wash and pat dry chickens. Mix salt, pepper, bay leaves, orange flavoring, and lime juice to a marinade. Coat chickens in marinade inside and outside. Allow to soak at room temperature for 30 minutes. Destone dates. Place in blender with pine nuts, marmalade and purée. Season purée with spices to create a savory taste.

Score kumquats and remove skin from physalis.

Sear spring chickens in hot, clarified butter on all sides for 4–6 minutes. Coat with marmalade mixture and place in a pre-moistened clay pot. Cover with fruit, sage leaves, and pour in stock. Cook chickens in a lidded clay pot in the oven for about 45 minutes at 390 °F/200 °C. After the meat is done, arrange chickens on plates. Remove sage leaves from pot, reserving 3 to purée with remaining juices for stock. Combine with yogurt to enrich flavor and add to spring chickens. Serve with a side order of pita bread.

Partridges in Champagne Sauce

Serves 4

4 prepared partridges
salt, pepper
1 cup/250 ml dry sparkling
Riesling or Champagne
2 tsp each rosemary and
thyme
3 tbsp freshly chopped
parsley
9 oz/250 g baby carrots
1 ⅔ cups/250 g peas
1 ⅔ cups/250 g pickling
onions
1 cup/250 g truffle butter
2 tbsp juniper berries
½ cup/125 ml mushroom
stock
1 oz/30 g marinated truffles

Preparation time: ca. 30 minutes
(plus marinating and
cooking time)
Per serving ca. 950 kcal/3990 kJ
59 g P, 67 g F, 21 g C

Wash and pat dry partridges, coat in salt and pepper and place in a bowl. Add sparkling wine or champagne to herbs and pour over partridges. Leave to marinate for 40 minutes.

Brush off and wash vegetables. Halve carrots. Peel onions. Stuff partridges with 1 oz/25 g each of truffle butter and juniper berries. Place breast-side up in a pre-moistened clay pot. Heat herb champagne with the remainder of truffle butter and pour over birds. Spread vegetables around meat. Close the lid and bake in oven for about 50 minutes at 390 °F/200 °C.

At the end of the cooking time, add mushroom stock and liquid from marinated truffles. Grate truffle over mixture and cook everything without the lid for a further 10–12 minutes.

Arrange partridges with vegetables on plates and serve. Mashed potato makes a tasty side order.

Serves 4

1 ¾ lb/800 g spring chicken breast

14 oz/400 g fresh button mushrooms

4 tbsp garlic oil

salt, pepper

2 cups/500 ml chicken stock

14 oz/400 g tomatoes with juice, canned

2 tsp each of crushed marjoram and thyme

2 ½ tbsp Cognac

14 oz/400 g precooked crayfish

1 bunch parsley

Spring Chicken Marengo

Preparation time: ca. 15 minutes
(plus cooking time)
Per serving ca. 698 kcal/2930 kJ
68 g P, 46 g F, 4g C

Wash and pat dry chicken and dice into about ¾ in/2 cm large chunks. Brush, rub clean and slice mushrooms.

Sear meat in hot garlic oil for 3–4 minutes. Add sliced mushrooms and braise for 2–3 minutes. Season with salt and pepper.

Place meat in a moistened clay pot and pour in chicken stock. Add tomatoes and herbs and stir well. Add more salt and pepper. Close lid and bake everything in the oven for 40 minutes at 390 °F/200 °C. Then add cognac and crayfish flesh and continue cooking for another 10–15 minutes.

Wash, dry and finely chop parsley. Serve chicken marengo with a garnish of chopped parsley. Fresh pita bread is a perfect side order.

Chicken Ratatouille

Peel and slice onions. Peel and finely chop garlic. Wash chicken, pat dry and cut into strips.

Sauté onions and garlic in hot olive oil for 3–4 minutes until glassy. Add chicken strips and continue frying for approximately 3–4 minutes.

Clean bell peppers, zucchini, and celery stalks, wash and dice into medium-size chunks. Wash tomatoes, remove stalks and slice flesh.

Place ⅓ of cooled chicken mixture into a moistened clay pot. Top with ⅓ of vegetables and season. Scatter with a sprinkling of herbs. Repeat this process until all the ingredients are used. Pour in stock and bake ratatouille in a lidded clay pot in the oven for 50 minutes at 390 °F/200 °C.

Serves 4

6 red onions

4 garlic cloves

1 lb 5 oz/600 g chicken breast, skinned and off bone

4 tbsp olive oil

2 yellow and 2 green bell peppers

12 oz/350 g zucchini, stick celery, and tomatoes

salt, pepper

1 tbsp crushed thyme

1 tbsp chopped basil

1 tsp crushed rosemary

½ cup/125 ml chicken stock

Preparation time: ca. 30 minutes (plus cooking time)
Per serving ca. 218 kcal/916 kJ
35 g P, 4 g F, 10 g C

Sweet and Sour Cooked Ham

Serves 4

14 oz/400 g cooked
ham joint

½ pineapple

1 large red chili

12 small potatoes

2 onions

4 sticks celery

1 pack puréed tomatoes
(ca. 14 oz/400 g)

1 cup/250 ml vegetable
stock

salt

freshly milled pepper

salt

1 pinch sugar

Preparation time: ca. 20 minutes
(plus cooking time)
Per serving ca. 288 kcal/1208 kJ
28 g P, 5 g F, 31 g C

Dice cooked ham. Peel and also dice pineapple. Scrub, wash and de-seed chilies, cutting flesh into rings. Peel potatoes, leaving them whole.

Peel and cut onions into rings, clean celery sticks, wash, dry and slice finely.

Layer all ingredients in a well-moistened clay pot, add puréed tomatoes and stock and mix. Season to a tangy taste with salt, pepper and sugar. Close lid and cook in oven at 390 °F/200 °C for about 60 minutes.

Spicy Spareribs

Divide spareribs into individual portions. Season with hickory smoke salt and pepper. Sear in heated peanut oil, ensuring the meat is evenly cooked, then set aside.

Peel and finely chop onions and garlic. Sauté in heated olive oil for about 3–4 minutes.

Add apple and cranberry juice, apple vinegar, tomato purée, sugar, mustard, horseradish, Worcestershire sauce, and paprika paste and allow sauce to simmer gently for about 5 minutes.

Season sauce liberally with salt and cayenne pepper. Place spareribs in a pre-moistened clay pot, covering alternately with sauce. Bake in oven in the open pot for about 70–80 minutes at 390 °F/200 °C.

Arrange spareribs on a platter and top with sauce. Potato or mixed salad on the side complements this meal.

Serves 4

4 ½ lb/2 kg spareribs
hickory smoke salt,
(ready-mixed)
pepper
6 tbsp peanut oil
9 oz/250 g onions
4 garlic cloves
4 tbsp olive oil
1 cup/250 ml each of apple
and cranberry juice
4 tbsp apple vinegar
9 oz/250 g tomato purée
2–3 tbsp cane sugar
2–3 tbsp sweet mustard
1 tbsp each horseradish,
Worcestershire sauce, and
paprika paste
salt
cayenne pepper

Preparation time: ca. 25 minutes
(plus cooking time)
Per serving ca. 840 kcal/3528 kJ
69 g P, 32 g F, 42 g C

Serves 4

2 ¼ lb/1 kg beef goulash

4 tbsp clarified butter

2 tbsp hot curry powder

6 shallots

6 tbsp mango chutney

2 cups/500 ml instant
Asia stock

½ tbsp each ground pepper,
ginger, and garlic

12 oz/350 g potatoes

12 oz/350 g sweet-and-
sour pickled pumpkin

10 tbsp natural yogurt

Preparation time: ca. 20 minutes
(plus cooking time)
Per serving ca. 390 kcal/1638 kJ
29 g P, 19 g F, 26 g C

Beef Curry

Sear beef in hot, clarified butter for about 4–6 minutes. Then sprinkle with curry powder and sauté for a further 3–4 minutes.

Place meat in a well soaked clay pot. Peel and roughly chop shallots. Combine with mango chutney, Asia stock, pepper, ginger, and garlic powder and pour over meat. Bake in oven at 390 °F/200 °C for about 50–60 minutes.

Peel and dice potatoes. Place pumpkin pieces in a sieve and drain thoroughly. Add both ingredients to the meat about 15 minutes before the end of required cooking time.

To enrich curry flavor add yogurt, arrange and serve.

Veal Steak in Sauce

Wash and dry off veal steak. Halve onions. Grate limes. Peel and dice carrots and celery.

Heat oil in a skillet and sear meat. Remove and place in a pre-moistened clay pot. Mix vegetables with grated lime zest and toss in meat fat for about 4–5 minutes. Then pour evenly over meat.

Add veal stock and wine. Add bay leaf, allspice, mustard seeds, and lemon pepper, cook in a lidded pot at 430 °F/220 °C for about 2 hours and then allow to cool.

Drain stock, reserving 2–3 ¼ cups/500–750 ml. Whisk egg yolks with olive oil. Chop anchovies, drain and flake tuna fish. Fold both ingredients into egg mixture and combine with lemon juice. Add capers and season sauce with salt, pepper and sugar to create a spicy flavor. Slice meat and arrange on plates. Top with tuna sauce and garnish with parsley.

Serves 4

3 lb 5 oz/1 ½ kg veal steak, leg joint
1 ⅔ cups/200 g pickled onions
4–5 untreated limes
3 carrots
½ celery root
6–8 tbsp oil
2 cups/500 ml veal stock
2 cups/500 ml dry white wine
2 bay leaves
1 tbsp each allspice and mustard seeds
1–2 tbsp lemon pepper
3 egg yolks
1 cup/¼ l olive oil
6 anchovies
14 oz/400 g tuna fish in oil, canned
3 tbsp lemon juice
4 tbsp capers
1 tsp sugar
salt and pepper
4 tbsp chopped parsley

Preparation time: ca. 30 minutes (plus cooking time)
Per serving ca. 1078 kcal/4526 kJ
113 g P, 49 g F, 21 g C

Slovenian Lamb Stew

Serves 4

12 oz/350 g bacon pieces
8 shallots
8 red onions
3 garlic cloves
2 lb/900 g lamb shoulder,
off bone
1 lb 2 oz/500 g turnip
salt
pepper
2–3 tbsp crushed marjoram
1–2 tsp caraway seeds
1 quart/1 l lamb stock
1–2 tbsp apple vinegar
1 ¼ cups/250 g brown rice
3 red bell peppers
2 yellow bell peppers
1 bunch parsley
1 cup rice
7 oz/200 g tomato purée
hot ground paprika
noble sweet paprika
1 ½ tbsp Slivovitz

Preparation time: ca. 15 minutes
(plus cooking time)
Per serving ca. 850 kcal/3570 kJ
98 g P, 16 g F, 75 g C

Sear bacon pieces in a frying pan until lightly browned. Remove and set aside.

Peel and finely chop onions and garlic cloves. Dice meat and sear all over in bacon fat. Add onions and garlic and sauté 4–5 minutes, stirring occasionally. Place everything, including bacon pieces in a well-soaked clay pot.

Wash, peel and finely dice turnips and spread over meat. Sprinkle everything with marjoram and cumin and season to a spicy taste. Mix half lamb stock with vinegar and pour in. Cover pot and place in a cold oven, leaving to bake for about 90 minutes at 390 °F/200 °C.

Brush off, halve, de-seed, wash and finely chop bell peppers. Wash, dry and finely chop parsley.

Wash rice thoroughly. After 40 minutes of set cooking time, stir bell peppers, rice and tomato purée into meat and pour in remaining stock. Season stew to a spicy taste, stir well and finish cooking. 5 minutes before the end of cooking pour in Slivovitz and allow to simmer without the lid. Remove lamb stew from the oven and serve immediately.

Potato and Chicken Stew

Serves 4

4 chicken breasts,
skinned and off bone

salt

pepper

3 tbsp clarified butter

3 tbsp olive oil

2 bunch spring onions

1 lb 11 oz/750 g potatoes

2 cups/500 ml poultry stock

Preparation time: ca. 20 minutes
(plus cooking time)
Per serving ca. 393 kcal/1649 kJ
47 g P, 9 g F, 30 g C

Wash, rub dry and season chicken. Heat clarified butter with olive oil and sear meat on each side for 3–4 minutes. Set aside.

Clean spring onions, wash and slice into thin rings. Wash, peel and grate potatoes into thin slices.

Add half potatoes to moistened clay pot. Season with salt and pepper and add half the onions. Top with a layer of meat. Cover with remaining onions and potatoes and season.

Pour in stock. Cook the stew, lidded, in the oven for about 60 minutes at 390 °F/200 °C. Remove potato and chicken stew from oven, arrange on plates and serve immediately. Fresh salad complements the meal.

Mullet with Chard

Blanch chard leaves in boiling water for about 2 minutes, allow to drain and lay out on a work surface. Press thick stalks until flattened.

Finely chop tomatoes. Wash, shake dry and finely chop herbs. Wash fish, pat dry and dice into small chunks.

Mix onions with tomatoes, fish and herbs. Stir in Bottarga (measuring out carefully, as it is heavily salted) and combine well. Spread mass over chard leaves, folding the leafy side on top of each other and rolling up. Fasten with a wooden skewer.

Place rolls in a moistened clay pot, drizzle with garlic oil. Close lid and bake rolls for 45–50 minutes in oven at 390 °F/200 °C. Remove, arranging mullet on plates to serve.

Serves 4

16 chard leaves
3 ½ oz/100 g dried tomatoes
½ bunch basil
1 bunch parsley
1 lb 11 oz/750 g mullet fillet
9 oz/250 g onions in oil
3–4 tbsp Bottarga (air-dried roe, Sardinian specialty)
4 tbsp garlic oil

Preparation time: ca. 25 minutes (plus cooking time)
Per serving ca. 273 kcal/1145 kJ
40 g P, 9 g F, 7 g C

Bay Leaf Mussels

Serves 4

4 ½ lb/2 kg fresh blue mussels

4 fresh bay leaf sprigs

2 large onions

8 tbsp olive oil

½ tbsp freshly chopped rosemary

1 lb 5 oz/600 g peeled tomatoes, with juice from can

1 cup/250 ml rosé wine

1 cup/250 ml lobster stock

lime quarters for garnish

Preparation time: ca. 20 minutes (plus cooking time)
Per serving ca. 423 kcal/1775 kJ
52 g P, 8 g F, 25 g C

Wash mussels, allow to drain and discard any shells already open. Wash and shake dry bay leaf sprigs. Place in a pre-soaked clay pot.

Cover mussels with peeled and thinly sliced onions. Heat olive oil and sauté rosemary, stirring occasionally, for 3–4 minutes. Add peeled tomatoes in juice and braise everything for another 3–4 minutes.

Pour braising juices over mussels. Add wine and lobster stock. Allow to bake in the oven in a lidded pot for about 35–40 minutes at 390 °F/200 °C.

Drain mussels, reserving juices. Remove herb sprigs and any unopened mussel shells. Prize out mussel flesh, place in a dish with sauce and serve immediately. Pumpernickel or rye bread and butter are a tasty side order.

Serves 4

3 lb 5 oz/1 ½ kg cockles,
round or soft clams
4 onions
4 carrots
4 wild parsnips
4 celery sticks
1 cup/250 ml dry
white wine
1 cup/250 ml vegetable
stock
2 bay leaves
½ tbsp each allspice and
peppercorns
2–3 tbsp untreated,
grated lemon zest
2 tbsp each celery and
fennel seeds
salt, pepper
3–4 sprigs thyme

Clam Chowder

Preparation time: ca. 30 minutes
(plus cooking time)
Per serving ca. 305 kcal/1281 kJ
33 g P, 4 g F, 29 g C

Wash mussels and discard any opened shells. Peel and dice onions. Scrub, wash, peel and also dice carrots, parsnips and stick celery.

Place mussels in a pre-soaked clay pot. Add vegetables, pour in wine and stock. Add bay leaves and spicy peppercorns, seasoning everything to a tangy taste with lemon zest, celery and fennel seeds, salt and pepper. Wash and shake dry thyme sprigs and place in pot.

Cover the clay pot and bake everything for 35–40 minutes at 375 °F/ 190 °C. At the end of the required cooking time, remove thyme, discarding any unopened shells. Clam chowder is best served with crispy baguette or rice.

Pike with Asparagus

Wash and pat dry pike fillets, drizzle with lemon juice and season with salt and pepper. Brush off and wash sugar snaps. Wash, peel and cut asparagus lengthways into 1 ½–2 ¼ in/ 4–5 cm slices.

Blanch vegetables in hot vegetable stock for 3–6 minutes. Blend crab butter with stock. Season everything to taste with salt, pepper and nutmeg.

Place stock with vegetables in a pre-soaked clay pot. Top with pike fillets. Wash and shake dry lemon grass and scatter over fish fillets. Close the lid and cook everything in the oven for about 35–40 minutes at 355 °F/180 °C.

At the end of the required cooking time, remove lemon grass. Arrange fish with vegetables and serve with a side order of potatoes.

Serves 4

4 pike fillets
(à 9 oz/250 g each)
2 tbsp lemon juice
salt and pepper
generous 1 lb/500 g sugar
snaps
generous 1 lb/500 g
asparagus
generous 1 ½ cups/375 ml
vegetable stock
14 tbsp crab butter
½ tsp ground nutmeg
4–5 spears lemon grass

Preparation time: ca. 15 minutes
(plus cooking time)
Per serving ca. 512 kcal/2150 kJ
19 g P, 46 g F, 6 g C

Sweet Bulgur Wheat Platter

Serves 4

10 ½ oz/300 g strawberries

10 ½ oz/300 g nectarines

10 ½ oz/300 g pears

10 ½ oz/300 g kiwi

2 ½ cups/350 g bulgur wheat

1 cinnamon stick

1 cup/250 ml milk

4 tbsp maple syrup

3 tbsp fig preserve

4–6 tbsp rum

1 bunch lemon grass

Preparation time: ca. 20 minutes (plus simmering and cooking time)
Per serving ca. 478 kcal/2006 kJ
12 g P, 4 g F, 94 g C

Wash strawberries, removing stalks. Wash, halve and remove pips from nectarines. Wash, quarter and remove pear cores. Peel kiwis.

Mix bulgur wheat with cinnamon stick, 2 cups/500 ml water, milk, maple syrup and fig preserve. Place in a well-soaked clay pot and bake bulgur wheat in the lidded pot in oven for approximately 35–45 minutes at 355 °F/180 °C.

Cut fruit into small pieces and drizzle with rum. Wash lemon grass, shake dry and finely chop. Add to fruit, stirring in gently. Allow fruit mixture to marinate for 20–30 minutes.

Turn off oven after cooking and remove pot. Loosen bulgur wheat with a fork and remove cinnamon stick. Stir fruit mixture into bulgur wheat and allow to cook gently in the warm oven without the lid for a further 8–12 minutes. Arrange bulgur wheat and fruit salad on a tepid platter and serve.

Baked Bananas

Finely chop cashew nuts and ginger.

Peel and thickly slice bananas and place in a pre-soaked clay pot. Drizzle with lemon juice.

Top with nuts and ginger. Then sprinkle with spices and coconut flakes. Close lid and bake bananas for about 30–35 minutes in oven at 355 °F/180 °C.

Remove baked bananas, arrange on a plate and serve with a garnish of mint leaves. Chocolate sauce or honey is a perfect accompaniment.

Serves 4

scant 2 cups/200 g
unsalted cashew nuts
9 oz/250 g candied ginger
4 bananas, uniform size
2 tbsp lemon juice
1 knife tip each cardamom,
ground cloves, and aniseed
7 oz/200 g coconut flakes
mint leaves for garnish

Preparation time: ca. 15 minutes
(plus cooking time)
Per serving ca. 720 kcal/3024 kJ
13 g P, 53 g F, 48 g C

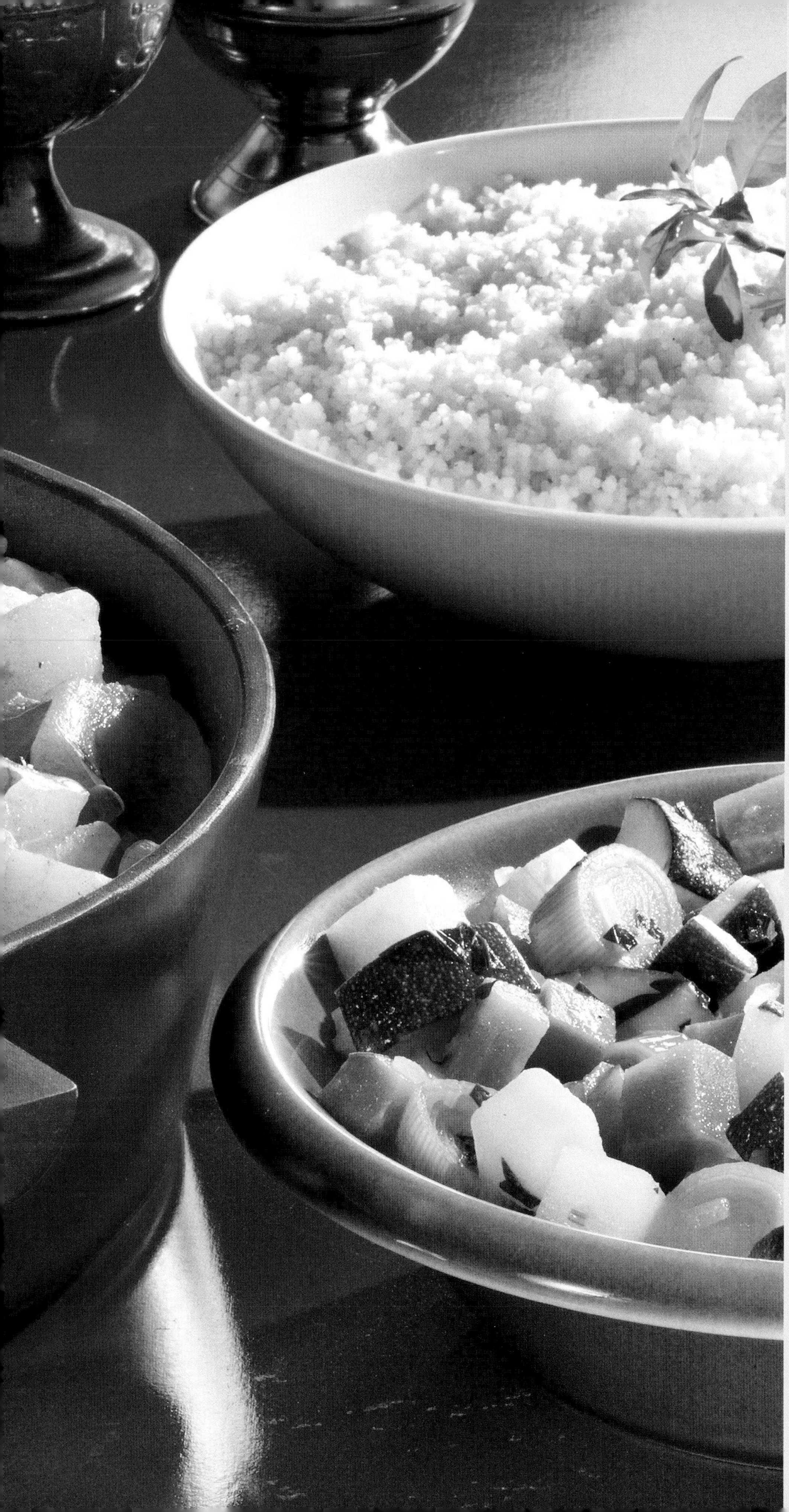

Tagine

The Tagine

One of the most important kitchen utensils in North African cuisine – especially the Maghreb states of Morocco, Tunisia and Algeria – is the tagine. The authentic dish consists of a thick, flat pot made out of clay, which can be sealed with a lid that rises upwards in a skittle form. This original tagine (often spelt Tajin) was modified by IKEA and adapted to a modern lifestyle, so that it can also be used in up-to-date electric ovens. The advantages of cooking in the tagine are carefully preserved: various ingredients cook slowly and gently together in one pot, in which a steady condensation of vapors forming in the high lid produces an intensity of flavors, giving tagine-prepared dishes their unique and aromatic quality.

The conserved heat only emits gradually so that the meal simmers away gently for a while, even after the oven is switched off. In this

way, wonderful sauces are created over the cooking times that require no extra preparation. A tagine is the nearest thing to a braising dish or stew pot. However, neither of these has the pointed lid of a tagine and therefore does not produce the condensed vapors, which percolate around the ingredients at regular intervals. In addition to the tagine as a utensil, it is also the name for a method of preparation. Meat is seared in oil and seasoned. The remaining ingredients, mostly vegetables or dried fruit, are placed over the meat, seasoned and then steamed in the closed pot. Liquid is added in the form of stock or water and is topped up during cooking, as required. An important tip: the tagine does not require stirring.

Fish is prepared a little differently. For one thing, hard vegetables, such as carrots, are placed in the pot so that none of the fish sticks to the sides, breaking up upon removal. For another, it is not necessary to fry the fish.

Tagine – Spices and Sauces

Especially exotic spices are used for seasoning. For the yellowish "m'qalli" sauce, the dish is seasoned with saffron threads and ginger. Both spices are sautéed in oil, before adding the meat. Whilst gently roasting, the saffron slowly emits its taste. "G'dra" sauce also has a yellowish hue, created by saffron and pepper; in addition, butter and sautéed onions enhance the flavor. For "M'schmermel" sauce, the ingredients are lightly braised in various spices, such as paprika, coriander, saffron, cumin and ginger. This sauce is also based on onions sautéed in butter or oil. There are also special Moroccan spice mixes or the spicy hot harissa paste made from chili, cumin and olive oil that are always at hand. Fresh herbs, such as parsley or coriander, are naturally also used for seasoning.

Side Orders

The finished tagine is served as it comes at the table. In Morocco, a tagine is eaten directly from the pot with a side order of bread. This means that the larger meat chunks are broken up with the fingers, with the bread being used afterwards to soak up the sauce. Pita bread is therefore served with every tagine. In restaurants or at major festivals, there is also rice or couscous. This coarsely ground wheat semolina is prepared in a special pot known as "keskes". This is a cooking pot with an inset sieve in which the couscous cooks in steam. But if you want to prepare couscous, you can also do this in a normal saucepan, in which you suspend a sieve. If your curiosity is now aroused by this delicious method of preparation, we have put together some typical North African dishes for you, which you can prepare at home in the new stylish tagine.

Beef with Chick Peas

Serves 4

3 tbsp olive oil

1 garlic clove

1 fresh ginger root
(¾ in/2 cm)

1 knife tip saffron powder

½ tsp cumin

½ tsp ground paprika,
noble sweet

2 cans chopped tomatoes
(4 ½ cups/850 g)

salt, pepper

2 lb 3 oz/1 kg beef goulash

1 large onion

generous 1 lb/500 g
zucchini

2 cans chick peas
(2 ⅛ cups/425 g each)

½ bunch freshly chopped
flat leaf parsley

2 ½ tbsp butter

Preparation time: ca. 20 minutes
(plus cooking and braising time)
Per serving: ca. 865 kcal/3633 kJ
69 g P, 41 g F, 54 g C

Heat 2 tbsp oil in a pot. Peel and chop garlic and ginger and sauté in oil. Add canned tomatoes with juice. Season sauce to taste with spices and allow braising for about 15 minutes.

Grease base of the tagine dish with remaining oil. Season meat. Peel and dice onion. Clean zucchini and cut into chunks. Place chick peas in a sieve, rinse with cold water and leave to drain thoroughly.

Spread vegetables over meat and cover with tomato sauce. Close tagine lid and braise meat over a medium heat for about 1 hour 20 minutes. Sprinkle finished dish with parsley and butter flakes and serve.

Lamb Tagine with Apricots

Peel and chop onions. Heat 2 tbsp olive oil in tagine and sauté onions. Clean lamb and dice in bite size chunks. Add to onions and sear all over. Add saffron threads, cinnamon, coriander and cumin, mix everything thoroughly and pour in vegetable stock.

Cover tagine and steam dish over a medium heat for about 50 to 60 minutes, until the fish is soft. Meanwhile, halve dried apricots, place in tagine and cook everything for a further 5 minutes.

Bring 2 cups/500 ml water to a boil with a little salt. Remove pot from heat and stir in couscous. Add butter in flakes and cook everything over low heat for 3 minutes, lifting couscous with a fork. Serve couscous with lamb tagine.

Serves 4

2 onions
3 tbsp olive oil
1 lb 5 oz/600 g lamb
a few saffron threads
1 tsp ground cinnamon
1 tsp ground coriander
1 tsp ground cumin
3 ¼ cups/750 ml vegetable stock
7 oz/200 g dried apricots
7 oz/200 g couscous
1 ½ tbsp butter

Preparation time: ca. 20 minutes
(plus frying and cooking time)
Per serving: ca. 550 kcal/2310 kJ
49 g P, 19 g F, 44 g C

Serves 4

2 lb 3 oz/1 kg mutton
or lamb
2 onions
1 garlic clove
5 tbsp clarified butter
1 pinch saffron powder
1 tsp ground ginger
2 tbsp olive oil
3 ¼ cups/750 ml meat
stock
15 artichoke hearts
1 bunch freshly chopped
coriander
1 preserved lemon
1 ¾ oz/50 g black olives

Preparation time: ca. 30 minutes
(plus frying and cooking time)
Per serving: ca. 490 kcal/2058 kJ
75 g P, 19 g F, 4 g C

Lamb Tagine with Artichokes

Clean and dice meat. Peel and chop onions and garlic. Heat clarified butter in tagine and sauté meat all over. Add onions and garlic and stir in spices.

Drizzle pot with oil and drench with stock. Allow cooking for about 1 hour.

Let artichoke hearts drain and place over meat. Sprinkle with chopped coriander and allow everything to braise for another 20 minutes, until the meat is very tender.

5 minutes before serving, slice marinated lemon in strips and scatter over meat with olives.

Vegetable Tagine

Peel and dice potatoes, kohlrabi and carrots. Clean and cut zucchini into pieces. Thoroughly clean leeks and chop into rings. Peel and chop onions and garlic.

Heat 1 tbsp oil in a tagine and sauté garlic. Add chopped vegetables and braise for a while, stirring occasionally. Add stock and simmer vegetables for about 15 minutes.

Heat remaining oil in a pan and sauté onions with chopped chili, cumin and parsley. Stir mixture into vegetables and cook for a further 5 minutes. Serve with rice or couscous.

Serves 4

4 potatoes
2 kohlrabi
4 carrots
4 zucchini
3 leeks
3 garlic cloves
2 onions
2 tbsp olive oil
1 quart/1 l vegetable stock
1 red chili
1 tsp ground cumin
½ bunch freshly chopped
flat leaf parsley

Preparation time: ca. 30 minutes
(plus braising and cooking time)
Per serving: ca. 197 kcal/827 kJ
10 g P, 4 g F, 28 g C

Tagine with Pumpkin

Serves 4

1 red onion

3 garlic cloves

1 tsp each ground cinnamon, cumin, and coriander

salt, pepper

1 tsp ground ginger

½ tsp cayenne pepper

3 carrots

2 red bell peppers

12 oz/350 g carrots

generous 1 lb/500 g pumpkin flesh, 2 different varieties

1 ¼ cups/250 g chick peas, canned

6 tbsp olive oil

15 dried apricots

1 tbsp tomato paste

2 cups/500 ml vegetable stock

1 pinch ground saffron

3 tbsp freshly chopped coriander leaves

Preparation time: ca. 30 minutes (plus braising and cooking time)
Per serving: ca. 303 kcal/1273 kJ
9 g P, 10 g F, 42 g C

Peel onions and garlic cloves, cut onions into rings. Chop garlic. Peel and quarter carrots, clean and dice paprika. Peel sweet potatoes and pumpkin and cut into bite size pieces. Allow chick peas to drain.

Heat 3 tbsp olive oil in tagine and sauté onions, garlic, cinnamon, cumin, and coriander for 3 minutes, stirring occasionally. Add carrots and paprika and sauté together for 2 minutes. Add potato and diced pumpkin to mixture and braise everything for another 3 minutes. Stir in chick peas, apricots, and tomato paste.

Pour in 2 cups/500 ml vegetable stock and bring mixture to a boil. Stir in saffron and cook lidded for about 20 minutes. Season to taste with salt and serve with a sprinkling of coriander. Serve with couscous.

Serves 4

1 dressed chicken

½ tsp each noble sweet ground paprika and ground cumin

pepper

1 lb 11 oz/750 g onions

4 tbsp peanut oil

a few saffron threads

3 ¼ cups/750 ml chicken stock

10 tbsp chick peas, canned

½ bunch freshly chopped parsley

1 tbsp fresh lemon thyme

1 ¼ cups/250 g rice

Preparation time: ca. 20 minutes (plus braising and cooking time)
Per serving: ca. 603 kcal/2533 kJ
39 g P, 21 g F, 64 g C

Moroccan Chicken

Clean chicken and cut into 4–6 portions. Stir in salt, paprika, cumin, and pepper and rub into chicken pieces. Peel and slice onion in rings.

Heat butter in tagine and sauté onion rings. Add chicken pieces and sear well. Scatter in saffron, pour in chicken stock and cook chicken pieces in the lidded pot for about 1 hour. Stir in drained chick peas after 30 minutes. 10 minutes before the end of cooking time, add parsley and lemon thyme.

Meanwhile, cook rice according to the instructions on the packet and spoon onto plates. Top with chicken portions and pour over sauce.

Serves 4

1 dressed chicken
2 onions
3 ½ tbsp olive oil
2 cinnamon sticks
1 tsp turmeric
salt, pepper
1 tsp ground ginger
1 sprig freshly chopped
coriander
1 ¼ cups/300 ml chicken
stock
5 pears
3 ½ tbsp butter
4 tbsp sugar syrup
4 tsp rose water

Preparation time: ca. 20 minutes
(plus braising and cooking time)
Per serving: ca. 540 kcal/2268 kJ
32 g P, 32 g F, 33 g C

Chicken Tagine with Pears

Peel and chop onions: cut chicken into quarters. Heat oil in tagine and sauté onions with chicken portions.

Add cinnamon sticks, turmeric, salt, pepper, ginger and coriander and pour in stock. Cover and braise everything for about 40 minutes.

Peel pears, remove cores and cut into quarters. Caramelize the pears in melted butter with sugar syrup. After an interval of 30 minutes, add pears and rose water to chicken. Remove cinnamon sticks. Serve with a side order of rice.

Meat and Rice Balls

Serves 4

1 cup/200 g round grain rice

generous 1 lb/500 g ground lamb

1 tsp each ground cinnamon, hot paprika and, ground coriander

⅔ cup/150 g clarified butter

2 onions

¼ tsp ground saffron

pepper

2 cups/500 ml vegetable stock

3 zucchini

2 red bell peppers

2 tbsp lemon juice

Preparation time: ca. 20 minutes (plus braising and cooking time)
Per serving: ca. 640 kcal/2688 kJ
43 g P, 31 g F, 47 g C

Combine rice and ground meat with each other and stir in spices. Heat clarified butter in a saucepan. Shape rice mixture into balls with damp fingers and sauté all over in hot fat.

Peel and chop onions and lightly brown with rice balls. Add to tagine with saffron, pepper, and stock and allow everything to simmer for about 40 minutes.

Clean zucchini and bell pepper, cutting the zucchini into slices and bell pepper in rings. Stir in vegetables and lemon juice 15 minutes before the end of cooking.

Serves 4

2 ½ lb/1 kg beef
2 onions
salt, pepper
½ tsp noble sweet ground paprika
3 ¼ cups/750 ml meat stock
1 sprig freshly chopped coriander
½ tsp ground saffron
½ tsp ground ginger
generous 1 lb/500 g quince
6 tbsp clarified butter
3 ½ oz/100 g dates, pitted

Preparation time: ca. 20 minutes
(plus cooking and braising time)
Per serving: ca. 659 kcal/2764 kJ
51 g P, 38 g F, 28 g C

Beef Tagine with Quince

Dice beef into bite size pieces. Peel and chop onions. Add meat and half diced onions to tagine, season with salt, pepper, and ground paprika and pour over stock. Bring to a boil, then stir in coriander, saffron and ginger.

Close tagine lid and allow everything to braise for about 60 minutes, until the meat is very soft. Meanwhile, peel and halve quinces, remove cores and cut flesh into bite size pieces.

Sauté quinces and remaining onions in clarified butter, until they are slightly browned. Half way into cooking, add quince, onions and dates to the meat. Season dish once more before serving.

Beef with Fruits

Dice meat into bite size pieces. Peel and chop onions. Mix together the olive oil, salt, pepper and spices well and carefully coat the meat with the mixture.

Place meat in tagine and sear in hot clarified butter. Add enough water to the meat. Cook lidded over a medium heat for about 60 minutes, until the meat is tender.

Meanwhile, soak dried fruits in boiling water. Ladle 2 spoons of stock into a small pan. Add half of the sugar, lemon zest and cinnamon stick. Add dried fruits and simmer for 20 minutes, until softened.

Add remaining sugar, dried fruits and stock to meat, and stir. Bring to a boil and reduce the meat sauce a little. Garnish with mint. Serve with a side order of bulgur wheat.

Serves 4

9 oz/750 g beef
2 large onions
3 tbsp olive oil
salt, pepper
1 tsp ground cinnamon
1 tsp freshly grated ginger
5 tbsp clarified butter
scant 4 cups/500 g mixed dried fruits
4 tbsp sugar
grated zest ½ untreated lemon
½ cinnamon stick
mint leaves for garnish

Preparation time: ca. 30 minutes
(plus braising and cooking time)
Per serving: ca. 695 kcal/2919 kJ
40 g P, 24 g F, 82 g C

Chicken Tagine with Peach

Serves 4

1 spring chicken,
ca. 3 lb 2 oz/1 ½ kg

4 tbsp olive oil

salt, pepper

1 pinch ground coriander

1 pinch ground cinnamon

½ tsp turmeric

2 garlic cloves

2 onions

2 carrots

½ bunch each freshly
chopped coriander and
parsley

generous 1 ⅔ cups/400 ml
chicken stock

2 peaches

2 tbsp rose water

1 tsp noble sweet ground
paprika

Preparation time: ca. 30 minutes
(plus braising and cooking time)
Per serving: ca. 330 kcal/1386 kJ
32 g P, 17 g F, 11 g C

Divide chicken into 4 to 6 portions. Heat oil in a skillet and lightly fry the chicken. Stir in spices, so they coat the meat.

Peel and chop garlic and onions. Peel and grate carrots. Add all the ingredients to chicken and stir in herbs. Pour in chicken stock and braise everything for about 50 minutes.

Drench peaches with hot water, removing skins. Halve fruits, removing stone and cutting the flesh into strips. Flavor with rose water and add to chicken 5 minutes before the end of cooking time. Serve the tagine with a sprinkling of paprika.

Chicken Tagine with Lentils

Peel and slice onion into rings. Drench tomatoes with boiling water, remove skin, stalk, seeds and then dice. Cut chicken into 4 – 6 portions.

Heat oil in a tagine or braising pot and sauté onion rings with tomatoes. Add chicken portions with spices and braise for about 6 minutes. Add 1 ½ quarts/1 ½ l water and stir in coriander. Cover and cook lidded for about 40 minutes, until meat is tender.

Wash lentils and allow to drain. Then add to tagine and braise everything for a further 30 minutes. Dice bread and roast until crisp along with the sesame seeds.

Serves 4

1 onion
1 tomato
1 chicken,
ca. 2 lb 1 oz/1 ¼ kg
2 tbsp olive oil
2 tsp pepper
1 tsp turmeric
1 ½ tsp salt
1 sprig freshly chopped coriander
3 tbsp black sesame seeds
⅔ cups/130 g lentils
10 ½ oz/300 g bread, from yesterday

Preparation time: ca. 30 minutes (plus cooking and roasting time)
Per serving: ca. 573 kcal/2407 kJ
43 g P, 21 g F, 51 g C

93

Serves 4

1 dressed chicken

1 onion

4 tbsp olive oil

2 tsp noble sweet ground paprika

½ tsp ground ginger

½ tsp black pepper

1 cup/250 ml chicken stock

8 saffron threads

1 sprig coriander

2 bunches parsley

1 tbsp lemon juice

2 preserved lemons

Preparation time: ca. 30 minutes (plus braising and cooking time)
Per serving: ca. 350 kcal/1470 kJ
31 g P, 20 g F, 9 g C

Lemon Chicken

Divide chicken into 4 to 6 portions. Peel onions and cut in rings. Heat oil in tagine and lightly brown chicken portions with paprika, ginger and pepper, until meat is coated in spices.

Add onion rings, stock, crushed saffron threads and bundled herbs and braise everything with the lid on for about 55 minutes.

Peel rind of preserved lemons and slice into strips. Press out 1 tbsp fruit flesh. Remove chicken from tagine and keep warm. Remove herbs from sauce and bring to a boil. Add lemon juice and fruit flesh and braise for 4 minutes. Stir in lemon peel. Serve lemon chicken with warm pita bread.

Chicken with Eggplant

Divide chicken into 6 portions. Peel and chop onions. Heat 3 tbsp oil in a frying pan and sauté onions. Add ginger and cinnamon and briefly cook. Add chicken pieces to frying pan and lightly brown. Pour in stock, crushed saffron and stir in herbs. Braise mixture with closed lid for about 50 minutes.

Clean and slice eggplant. Lay out and sprinkle with salt, allowing to soak for 20 minutes, then pat dry. Coat with remaining oil and, on a roasting tray, brown on each side under a warm grill for about 6 minutes. Soak tomatoes in warm water.

Remove cooked chicken pieces from roasting pan and keep warm. Bring the sauce to a boil and add sliced eggplant, reserving 10 portions. Let tomatoes drain, dice and cook with other ingredients for 5 minutes. Arrange chicken pieces with sauce and serve with crispy bread.

Serves 4

1 dressed chicken,
ca. 2 lb 10 oz/1 ¼ kg
2 onions
5 tbsp olive oil
2 tsp ground ginger
1 tsp ground cinnamon
1 cup/250 ml chicken stock
8 saffron threads
½ sprig freshly chopped coriander
½ bunch freshly chopped parsley
2 eggplant
15 dried tomatoes
salt, pepper

Preparation time: ca. 30 minutes
(plus braising, grilling
and cooking time)
Per serving: ca. 333 kcal/1399 kJ
33 g P, 18 g F, 10 g C

Quails in Paprika Sauce

Serves 4

2 cups/500 ml chicken stock

12 saffron threads

½ cup/100 g couscous

2 tbsp roasted and chopped pine nuts

5 tbsp freshly chopped flat leaf parsley

2 tsp dried oregano

2 tsp clarified butter

2 tbsp olive oil

2 tsp noble sweet ground paprika

½ tsp ground cumin

2 onions

4 dressed quails

salt, pepper

4 tbsp freshly chopped coriander

4 tbsp butter

Preparation time: ca. 30 minutes (plus cooking, braising and frying time)
Per serving: ca. 450 kcal/1890 kJ
41 g P, 25 g F, 15 g C

Bring 1 cup/250 ml chicken stock and 4 saffron threads to a boil, stir in couscous. Reduce heat, cover pot and allow to braise for about 5 minutes. Combine with 1 tbsp pine nuts, 2 tbsp parsley, oregano and clarified butter. Season to taste with salt.

Blend olive oil with remaining saffron, paprika and cumin. Peel and chop onions. Coat quails in the mixture. Rub salt and pepper inside and stuff with couscous mixture.

Place quails alongside each other in a tagine, arranging remaining parsley, onions and coriander around the meat. Pour in remaining chicken stock. Close lid of tagine and braise quails for about 30 minutes. Then remove from tagine.

Heat butter and sear quails until crisp on the outside. Bring the sauce to a boil and stir in remaining pine nuts. Arrange quails and serve with sauce.

Serves 4

3 onions

2 garlic cloves

6 tomatoes

1 red chili

1 lb 5 oz/600 g ground meat

½ bunch freshly chopped parsley

2 tbsp tomato paste

1 tsp ginger

salt, pepper

2 tbsp olive oil

generous ¾ cup/200 ml fish stock

1 tsp harissa paste

3 eggs

Mincemeat Tagine

Preparation time: ca. 20 minutes (plus braising and cooking time)
Per serving: ca. 475 kcal/1995 kJ
36 g P, 34 g F, 7 g C

Peel and chop onions and garlic. Remove stalks from tomatoes and dice. Clean and chop chili. Knead the mincemeat into a dough together with the onions, half the garlic, chili, ginger, salt, pepper and parsley. Form small spheres and set aside.

Sauté remaining onions in hot olive oil until glassy. Add tomatoes and remaining garlic and braise everything for about 3 minutes. Stir in tomato paste and pour in stock. Season with salt, pepper and harissa paste. Add ground meat balls, close lid and allow to simmer for about 10 minutes.

Carefully slide eggs into the sauce, so that the yolk remains whole and simmer everything until the eggs turn solid. Serve with pita bread.

Serves 4

2 red bell peppers
1 onion
generous 1 lb/500 g
tomatoes
2 tbsp olive oil
salt, pepper
1 tsp sugar
2 tbsp capers
½ tsp harissa paste
4 eggs
3 ½ oz/100 g Feta

Preparation time: ca. 20 minutes
(plus braising and cooking time)
Per serving: ca. 224 kcal/941 kJ
14 g P, 15 g F, 8 g C

Tomato Omelet with Bell Pepper

Clean and chop bell peppers into strips. Peel and chop onions. Drench tomatoes in boiling water. Remove skin, stalks and de-seed and dice the flesh.

Heat oil in a pot and sauté onions. Add tomatoes and lightly fry with onions. Season to taste with salt, pepper and sugar. Allow to simmer for about 30 minutes, until mixture forms a thick sauce. Remove pot from heat.

Mix capers with harissa paste in 1 tbsp water and stir into sauce. Whisk eggs and also stir in. Crumble and add goat or Feta cheese.

Place strips of bell pepper in a pre-greased tagine and pour over egg mixture. Close the tagine lid and allow mixture to thicken for about 25 minutes over a medium heat.

Lamb Tagine with Fennel

Serves 4

2 red onions
2 garlic cloves
1 fennel root
2 tbsp oil
1 lb 11 oz/750 g lamb fillet
1 tsp cinnamon
2 tsp ground cumin
2 tsp ground coriander
½ tsp cayenne pepper
½ tsp salt
5 oz/150 g dates, pitted

Preparation time: ca. 30 minutes
(plus braising and cooking time)
Per serving: ca. 440 kcal/1848 kJ
57 g P, 10 g F, 29 g C

Peel onions and garlic. Chop onions into rings and slice garlic. Clean fennel removing hard external leaves and slice up the root. Dice meat into bite size pieces.

Heat oil in tagine and lightly fry onions, garlic and fennel, until everything is lightly browned. Remove and leave on a plate. Place lamb chunks in the pot and fry lightly.

Add spices and salt and sauté with other ingredients for about 1 minute. Add dates with fennel mixture and scant 2 cups/450 ml water and stir well. Allow to braise for about 90 minutes. Top up with water, as required. Serve with fried bread on the side.

Serves 4

1 ¾ lb/800 g beef
2 ¼ lb/1 kg tomatoes
3 tbsp olive oil
1 tbsp ground cumin
½ tsp pepper
7 oz/200 g green olives, pitted
4 garlic cloves
1 tbsp lemon juice
4 tbsp freshly chopped flat leaf parsley

Preparation time: ca. 40 minutes
(plus braising and cooking time)
Per serving: ca. 575 kcal/2415 kJ
43 g P, 40 g F, 11 g C

Beef Tagine with Olives

Dice meat into cubes measuring 1 ¼ in/3 cm. Drench tomatoes in boiling water, remove skins, stalks, de-seed and dice tomato flesh.

Heat oil in tagine and sear meat well all over. Peel garlic and scatter whole cloves around the meat. Close lid of tagine and cook for about 40 minutes. Then remove the meat and garlic from the tagine and keep warm.

Heat tomato sauce, add lemon juice and allow sauce to reduce a little. Pour over meat and serve with fresh bread.

Fish with Tomato Sauce

Mix olive oil, parsley, coriander, ground paprika, crushed saffron threads, ginger and lemon juice. Place fish fillets in marinade, so that everything is well coated. Allow to marinate for 2 hours, turning once.

Drench tomatoes in boiling water, remove skins, stalks, de-seed and chop the flesh. Peel and chop garlic. Peel onions and carrots and slice both ingredients, slicing the lemons as well.

Let tomatoes and garlic braise in a saucepan with cumin for about 10 minutes. Season to taste with salt and pepper. Cover the tagine with a layer of carrots. Arrange sliced onion on top and pour over tomato sauce. Close lid and leave to braise for about 20 minutes, until carrots are softened.

Arrange fish fillets over vegetables. Top with sliced lemon and pour over marinade, placing olives around mixture. Close lid and braise for 12 minutes, until the fish is done.

Serves 4

½ cup/125 ml olive oil
4 tbsp freshly chopped parsley
2 tbsp freshly chopped coriander
2 tsp noble sweet ground paprika
8 saffron threads
1 tsp ground ginger
½ lemon, juiced
4 fish fillets (each 5 oz/150 g)
4 tomatoes
2 garlic cloves
1 onion
2 carrots
1 untreated lemon
1 tsp ground cumin
salt, pepper
12 green olives

Preparation time: ca. 30 minutes
(plus braising and cooking time)
Per serving: ca. 355 kcal/1491 kJ
29 g P, 21 g F, 11 g C

Beef with Eggplant Purée

Serves 4

1 ¾ lb/800 g beef
1 onion
1 garlic clove
½ cup/125 ml oil
1 tsp pepper
1 pinch saffron powder
salt
3 ¼ cups/750 ml vegetable stock
1 ¾ lb/800 g eggplant
1 lemon, juiced
2 tomatoes
1 bunch freshly chopped flat leaf parsley

Preparation time: ca. 30 minutes
(plus braising, frying
and cooking time)
Per serving: ca. 475 kcal/1995 kJ
43 g P, 30 g F, 8 g C

Dice meat into bite size pieces. Peel and chop onions and garlic. Heat 2 tbsp oil in tagine and lightly fry onions and garlic. Stir in spices and lightly brown for a while, then add diced meat and sauté in the spice mixture. Pour in stock, close lid and allow everything to braise for about 50 minutes.

Clean eggplant and cut into ⅓ in/1 cm thick slices. Drizzle with lemon juice and allow to soak. Heat remaining oil in a skillet and lightly fry eggplant slices until soft. Remove from skillet, drain in kitchen towel, squash with a fork and keep warm.

Drench tomatoes in boiling water, remove skins, stalks, de-seed and dice the flesh. Add tomatoes to meat with parsley and allow everything to simmer for a further 15 minutes, until sauce has reduced a little. Pour eggplant purée over meat, then serve.

Tagine with Eggs

Drench tomatoes in boiling water, remove skins, stalks, de-seed and chop the flesh. Blanche olives in boiling water for about 1 minute. Drain and chop.

Heat oil in tagine. Peel and chop onions and garlic and sauté in hot oil with olives. Stir in honey and allow onions to caramelize. Add garlic, tomatoes and bay leaf and lightly fry, stirring occasionally. Reduce everything to a sauce in about 30 minutes. Remove bay leaf.

Whisk eggs with parsley, cumin, salt and pepper. Slowly add boiling tomato sauce and allow to solidify. Serve with a garnish of coriander. Fresh bread is a perfect side order for this dish.

Serves 4

3 tomatoes
20 green olives, pitted
2 tbsp olive oil
2 onions
2 garlic cloves
1 tsp honey
1 bay leaf
8 eggs
4 tbsp freshly chopped parsley
2 tsp ground cumin
salt, pepper
coriander for garnish

Preparation time: ca. 20 minutes
(plus braising and cooking time)
Per serving: ca. 300 kcal/1260 kJ
17 g P, 23 g F, 8 g C

Serves 4

generous 1 lb/500 g tomatoes

1 lb/450 g spinach

2 garlic cloves

5 tbsp clarified butter

1 tbsp noble sweet ground paprika

1 tsp turmeric

1 tsp cumin

⅔ cup/150 ml pint fish stock

1 ¾ lb/800 g sea pike

2 untreated lemons

salt, pepper

½ sprig freshly chopped parsley

generous ¾ cup/100 g slivered almonds

Preparation time: ca. 30 minutes (plus braising and cooking time)
Per serving: ca. 310 kcal/1302 kJ
42 g P, 10 g F, 10 g C

Fish Tagine with Almonds

Drench tomatoes in boiling water, remove skins and stalks, de-seed and dice the flesh. Clean and finely chop spinach. Peel and chop garlic.

Heat clarified butter in the tagine and lightly sweat garlic with spices. Add diced tomato and spinach, pour in fish stock and allow everything to simmer for about 15 minutes.

Cut fish into bite size pieces. Wash lemon in hot water and cut into quarters. Place fish pieces, lemons and tomatoes in the tagine, close lid and braise for about 20 minutes. Season cooked fish tagine as desired and serve with a garnish of parsley and slivered almonds.

Fish Tagine with Vegetables

Peel and chop onions and garlic. Mix thoroughly with spices, 5 tbsp parsley, coriander, 5 tbsp olive oil, half lemon juice, 2 tbsp water, 1 tsp salt and a little pepper. Score sea bream on both sides in a cross-cross pattern and coat with a third of vegetable mixture. Allow to marinate for about 60 minutes.

Peel red onion and cut into rings. Clean and slice celery. Peel potatoes, remove stalk from tomatoes and slice both ingredients. Heat remaining oil in a tagine and sauté onions. Add second third of spice mixture and continue frying.

Scatter onion rings over the base of the tagine. Layer vegetables, alternating between celery, potatoes and tomatoes. Season every layer with salt and pepper. Pour over remaining parsley and lemon juice. Mix remaining spice mixture with ½ cup/125 ml water and pour over vegetables.

Add olives and quartered, pickled lemons, bring to a boil and braise with the lid closed for about 10 minutes. Place fish on top of vegetables and cook everything for a further 25 minutes. Turn fish after 12 minutes and top up the liquid.

Serves 4

1 large onion
2 garlic cloves
1 tsp cumin
1 tsp noble sweet ground paprika
½ tsp cayenne pepper
8 saffron threads
1 sprig freshly chopped flat leaf parsley
5 tbsp freshly chopped coriander
7 tbsp olive oil
1 lemon, juiced
salt, pepper
2 prepared sea bream
1 red onion
9 oz/250 g celery sticks
9 oz/250 g potatoes
2 tomatoes
20 green olives, pitted
6 preserved (marinated) lemons

Preparation time: ca. 35 minutes
(plus braising and cooking time)
Per serving: ca. 368 kcal/1546 kJ
19 g P, 24 g F, 19 g C

Beef with Vegetables

Serves 4

1 lb 9 oz/700 g beef

2 onions

3 tbsp olive oil

1 tsp turmeric

10 saffron threads

1 sprig coriander

2 bunches parsley

2 cups/500 ml meat stock

generous 1 lb/500 g young carrots

15 dried tomatoes

3 zucchini

3 potatoes

salt, pepper

Preparation time: ca. 30 minutes
(plus braising and cooking time)
Per serving: ca. 415 kcal/1743 kJ
40 g P, 19 g F, 20 g C

Dice meat into bite size chunks. Peel and chop onions. Heat 2 tbsp oil in tagine and sear onions with meat. Add turmeric and crushed saffron threads and braise for 3 minutes.

Wash coriander and parsley, tie in bundles and add to other ingredients. Pour in meat stock.

Wash and score carrots and cut dried tomatoes into strips. Cover meat with half of tomatoes and close the lid of the tagine. Cook for about 60 minutes.

Clean and slice zucchini. Peel potatoes and cut into quarters. Add zucchini, potatoes and carrots to meat, close lid and allow everything to braise for a further 35 minutes. Season to taste with salt and pepper.

Heat remaining oil in a frying pan and lightly fry remaining tomatoes. Arrange beef with sauce and pour over fried vegetables.

Wok

The Wok

The wok is probably the best known utensil in the Asian kitchen. It was created more than 3,000 years ago, when a cooking utensil was needed, in which ingredients could easily be prepared over a solitary open fire – firewood was scarce. The final product turned into a truly versatile invention with a variety of cooking options. The wok caters for all cooking methods: boiling, braising and frying, as well as steaming and baking – anything's possible!

Preparation and Cooking

In Asian cookery, preserving food's color, texture, aroma and flavor is vital. Individual ingredients must also be carefully coordinated to harmonize and complement each other. Proper preparation often takes longer than the cooking process itself, which is generally very quick. Ingredients are chopped up finely to keep cooking time to a minimum, and marinating adds a special flavor to food. Ingredients with different cooking times are blanched or precooked to ensure everything is ready at the same time. Various herbs and spices are lightly sautéed to fragrance the oil for the next ingredients. Dried foods are soaked. Rather than discarding the liquid, it is reserved for seasoning. In the Orient, people tend to avoid raw food, although they eat fresh fruit. Everything is cooked in some way, even if very rapidly, to make the meals easier to digest.

Cooking Methods

Stir-frying

Stir-frying is probably the most popular cooking method. Ingredients are sautéed in a small amount of very hot oil, whilst they are constantly tossed around the pan. They cook within a few minutes, without losing any of their natural flavors or vitamins and nutrients. Meat becomes crispy and seared on the outside and juicy on the inside. Vegetables stay fresh and slightly crunchy.

Braising

Braising initially requires only a small quantity of ingredients that are sautéed or seared, then drenched in liquid and braised with the lid on. This cooking method is best suited to coarse meat.

Deep-frying

Ingredients are fried in hot oil, either raw or in batter. The wok is especially well suited to this method, as much less oil is needed for frying than for conventional methods. Deep-frying is dead easy in a wok, as long as the oil is hot enough. To test if the temperature is right for deep-frying, dip a wooden chopstick into the oil and wait for small bubbles to start appearing on it. Then you can start deep-frying food.

Steaming

Steaming is another classical cooking method in China. Ingredients are placed in moistened steaming baskets, which are then immersed with a small amount of liquid in a wok to steam. Whilst steaming, it's essential that the food does not come into contact with the liquid in the pot and that the wok is well covered. The water level must be checked at regular intervals to see if it needs to be topped up.

Simmering

Food can also be left to simmer gently in a wok. Soups and stews are created in a wok, first by lightly browning vegetables, then adding in the liquid. In the wok, everything simmers away gently, until tender.

Steamed Cucumbers

Serves 4

4 cucumbers
7 oz/200 g shallots
¼ bunch Thai garlic chive
2 tbsp vegetable oil
2 tbsp oyster sauce

Preparation time: ca. 15 minutes
Per serving ca. 123 kcal/513 kJ
5 g P, 7 g F, 11 g C

Wash and dry cucumbers. Halve lengthways, remove seeds and cut into ¾ in/2cm thick chunks. Peel, wash and thinly slice shallots. Wash and finely chop garlic chive.

Heat oil in wok, add shallots and sweat briefly. Then add cucumber pieces, season with oyster sauce and drench with approximately generous ¾ cup/200 ml water.

Place lid on wok and stew vegetables for about 3 minutes. Finally, stir in garlic chive and arrange cucumbers.

Bamboo Shoots with Alfalfa

Slice bamboo shoots diagonally. Wash, clean and de-seed bell peppers and cut into strips. Wash and shake dry coriander, remove leaves and chop finely.

Heat oil in wok, lightly brown bell pepper strips, and then add bamboo shoots.

Mix in shrimp paste and hoisin sauce, combine and continue cooking.

Finally, toss in alfalfa sprouts, quickly stir through and serve with a sprinkling of coriander leaves.

Serves 4

generous 1 lb/500 g bamboo shoots
2 red and 2 green bell peppers
1 sprig coriander
4 tbsp vegetable oil
3 ½ oz/100 g alfalfa sprouts
1 tbsp shrimp paste
2 tbsp hoisin sauce

Preparation time: ca. 25 minutes
Per serving ca. 146 kcal/611 kJ
6 g P, 11 g F, 6 g C

Steamed Zucchini Tartlets

Serves 4

3 large zucchini
1 tbsp finely grated ginger
4 tbsp shrimp paste
1 bunch coriander

Preparation time: ca. 30 minutes
Per serving ca. 41 kcal/172 kJ
5 g P, 1 g F, 3 g C

Clean, wash and dry zucchini and cut into very thin slices. Wash and shake dry coriander, remove and finely chop a few leaves. Mix ginger with shrimp paste and 2 tbsp water.

Line bamboo baskets with some of the coriander leaves. Spread zucchini slices with a little paste and layer to form tartlets (about 2 in/5 cm high).

Place zucchini tartlets in bamboo baskets and sprinkle with chopped coriander.

Heat water in wok, place bamboo baskets over it. Cover and steam for approximately 15 minutes.

Stuffed Tomatoes

Wash and dry tomatoes, cut off tops and scoop out middle. Remove outer leaves of cabbage and cut in two. Cut out stalk and chop leaves into fine strips. Peel and finely slice ginger.

Heat oil in wok. Place strips of cabbage in the wok and steam until soft with powdered ginger, hoisin sauce, and fish sauce. Stuff tomatoes with cabbage and place three tomatoes in each bamboo basket. Sprinkle with ginger pieces.

Heat a little water in the wok, placing the baskets on top of each other. Cover wok with a lid. After 10 minutes, exchange the top and bottom baskets, leaving to steam for a further 10 minutes.

Finally, drizzle tomatoes with coriander oil and sprinkle with finely chopped coriander leaves.

Serves 4

12 medium tomatoes
½ small white cabbage
⅔ cup/100 g ginger root
1 tbsp vegetable oil
2 tbsp ginger powder
1 tbsp hoisin sauce
2 tbsp fish sauce
a little coriander oil
½ bunch coriander

Preparation time: ca. 40 minutes
Per serving ca. 122 kcal/512 kJ
4 g P, 4 g F, 15 g C

119

Serves 4

9 oz/250 g rice noodles (thick)

5 oz/150 g shallots

½ bunch Thai basil

2 tbsp peanut oil

1 tbsp palm sugar

1 tbsp red curry paste

4 tbsp light soy sauce

1 can unsweetened coconut milk (1 ⅔ cup/400 ml)

1 ¼ cups/250 g peas

5 oz/150 g cherry tomatoes

2 ⅓ cups/300 g tofu cubes

Kaffir lime leaves

Preparation time: ca. 35 minutes
Per serving ca. 337 kcal/1412 kJ
21 g P, 10 g F, 47 g C

Rice Noodles with Tofu Curry

Cook rice noodles according to instructions on the packet, drain, rinse with cold water and set aside. Peel shallots and chop Thai basil roughly.

Heat oil in wok, and lightly sauté palm sugar and curry paste. Add shallots, drench with soy sauce, pour in some of the coconut milk, and leave to thicken.

Pour in remaining coconut milk and continue braising for about 10 minutes. Then add peas and cherry tomatoes to sauce, leaving to simmer gently for another 5 minutes.

Finally, add roughly chopped Thai basil, tofu cubes, and cooked rice noodles and warm through. Serve topped with finely chopped Kaffir lime leaves.

Serves 4

generous 1 lb/500 g
broccoli florets
10 ½ oz/300 g small white
eggplant
1 green mango
4 tbsp vegetable oil
1 tbsp palm sugar
1 tbsp green curry paste
2 tbsp fish sauce
4 tbsp oyster sauce
1 ½ cans unsweetened
coconut milk
(2 ½ cups/600 ml)

Preparation time: ca. 20 minutes
Per serving ca. 174 kcal/730 kJ
6 g P, 12 g F, 10 g C

Broccoli with Coconut Milk

Clean, wash and dry broccoli florets. Wash eggplant and remove stem. Peel mango and cut flesh into very fine strips.

Heat oil in wok and lightly brown palm sugar and curry paste.

Add broccoli and the small white, whole eggplant, quickly tossing them in oil.

Drench with fish and oyster sauce and pour in coconut milk, leaving to simmer for about 5 minutes. Finally, sprinkle mango pieces over curry just before serving.

Papaya in Satay Sauce

Serves 4

2 lb 3 oz/1 kg green papaya
3 red chilies
3 tbsp peanuts
1 bunch coriander
4 tbsp vegetable oil
2 tbsp peanut paste
2 tbsp fish sauce
1 tsp yellow curry paste
1 can unsweetened coconut milk
(1 ⅔ cups/400 ml)

Preparation time: ca. 25 minutes
Per serving ca. 258 kcal/1080 kJ
7 g P, 21 g F, 11 g C

Peel papaya, scoop out seeds and thinly slice flesh. Wash and dry chilies and cut into narrow rings. Roughly chop peanuts. Wash and shake dry coriander, pick off leaves, chopping half of them.

Heat oil in wok; add in papaya strips and gently sauté for about 5 minutes without browning.

Then add in peanut paste, season with fish sauce, add in curry paste and gently fry. Drench with coconut milk, and leave to simmer until most of the liquid has evaporated.

Mix in chopped coriander leaves, add chili rings and chopped peanuts, and serve with a sprinkling of coriander leaves.

Steamed Rice Balls

Cook basmati rice as per packet instructions and allow to cool. Peel and slice ginger. Wash and shake dry coriander, and finely chop leaves. Peel 1 and finely chop 3 shallots, sear until crispy in hot oil and remove. Combine with candied ginger and a little coriander for the filling.

Line bamboo baskets with coriander leaves and ginger slices. With damp hands, form cooked rice into small balls. Make a well in each one, adding in some filling and reshape into rice balls.

Place balls in bamboo baskets and sprinkle over remaining sliced shallot. Heat water in wok and place bamboo baskets on top. Cover and steam for 10 minutes. Drizzle some sweet and sour sauce over rice balls, serving remainder as a dip.

Serves 4

1 cup/200 g basmati rice
⅔ cup/100 g ginger root
1 bunch coriander
4 shallots
2 tbsp vegetable oil
2 tbsp chopped, candied ginger
6 tbsp sweet and sour sauce

Preparation time: ca. 40 minutes
Per serving ca. 207 kcal/866 kJ
5 g P, 6 g F, 32 g C

Egg Tandoori Rice

Serves 4

1 ¼ cups/250 g long grain rice

4 eggs

2 tbsp tandoori mixed spices

6 tbsp vegetable oil

14 oz/400 g soya sprouts

4 tbsp fish sauce

Preparation time: ca. 25 minutes
Per serving ca. 426 kcal/1783 kJ
16 g P, 24 g F, 34 g C

Cook long grain rice as per instructions on packet and set aside. Whisk eggs and mix in 1 tbsp tandoori mixed spices.

Heat oil in wok, toss in soya sprouts and then remove.

Turn up heat, add eggs and leave to scramble. Add cooked rice, sprinkle over remaining tandoori spices and season with fish sauce. Finally, add soya sprouts and mix everything thoroughly.

Rice with Shiitake Mushrooms

Cook rice according to packet instructions and leave on one side. Soak shiitake mushrooms in water.

Wash and dry bell peppers, halve and remove seeds. Cut into bite size chunks. Clean spring onions and halve lengthways, then wash, dry and cut into small pieces.

Heat oil in wok and lightly fry spring onions. Add bell pepper pieces and continue to fry. Drain shiitake mushrooms, dice if necessary, add to vegetables and lightly fry. Season with soy and fish sauce.

Finally, stir in cooked rice and continue to fry for a few minutes until steaming hot.

Serves 4

1 ¼ cups/250 g long grain rice
7 oz/200 g dried shiitake mushrooms
2 red bell peppers
1 bunch spring onions
4 tbsp vegetable oil
2 tbsp light soy sauce
2 tbsp fish sauce

Preparation time: ca. 25 minutes
Per serving ca. 365 kcal/1527 kJ
8 g P, 11 g F, 59 g C

Sweet and Sour Vegetables

Serves 4

generous 1 lb/500 g cauliflower

9 oz/250 g carrots

2 red, 2 yellow and 2 green bell peppers

9 oz/250 g pineapple

1 bunch coriander

4 tbsp vegetable oil

generous ¾ cup/200 ml tomato ketchup

4 tbsp honey

2 tbsp rice vinegar

3 tbsp soy sauce

Preparation time: ca. 30 minutes
Per serving ca. 345 kcal/1443 kJ
8 g P, 11 g F, 52 g C

Wash and dry cauliflower and separate into florets. Clean, wash and peel carrots, and cut into ½ in/1 cm cubes. Wash, dry, de-seed and dice bell peppers. Peel pineapple and cut into ½ in/1 cm cubes. Wash and shake dry coriander, remove leaves and chop coarsely.

Heat oil in wok, sauté cauliflower florets and then remove. Sauté diced carrot in the same way, add bell peppers and pineapple, and continue frying. Then return cauliflower florets to wok.

Pour in tomato ketchup, honey, rice vinegar, soy sauce, and 1 cup/ 250 ml water, and leave to simmer gently for about 5 minutes, stirring regularly. Finally, stir in coarsely chopped coriander leaves.

Fried Green Beans

Wash and clean beans. Remove top leaves from leeks. Halve and wash leeks thoroughly, and cut into 1 ¼ in/3 cm pieces. Soak Mu Err mushrooms in water. Wash, dry and finely chop Thai garlic chive.

Heat oil in wok. Sweat beans in oil, add fish and oyster sauce and fry lightly. Add leek portions and drench with water if needed.

Drain Mu Err mushrooms and divide any large pieces, as necessary. Add mushrooms and shrimp to beans, pour in sweet and sour sauce and mix well. Stir in Thai garlic chive to finish.

Serves 4

1 lb 12 oz/800 g fine green beans
4 leeks
7 oz/200 g dried Mu Err mushrooms
¼ bunch Thai garlic chive
4 tbsp vegetable oil
2 tbsp fish sauce
2 tbsp oyster sauce
7 oz/200 g small shrimp
6 tbsp sweet and sour sauce

Preparation time: ca. 30 minutes
Per serving ca. 299 kcal/1254 kJ
22 g P, 13 g F, 22 g C

Lamb with Hoisin Sauce

Serves 4

generous 1 lb/500 g lamb shank

4 tbsp hoisin sauce

10 ½ oz/300 g shallots

4 tbsp vegetable oil

1 tsp five-spice powder

1 tsp palm sugar

2 tbsp rice vinegar

1 bunch coriander

Preparation time: ca. 15 minutes
(plus marinating time)
Per serving ca. 426 kcal/1784 kJ
38 g P, 27 g F, 3 g C

Wash meat, pat dry and cut into chunks. Mix with hoisin sauce and marinate for 30 minutes. Peel, halve and cut shallots lengthways into strips.

Heat half oil in wok; sauté shallots with five-spice powder for about 3 minutes until transparent, then remove.

Sear lamb pieces in remaining sizzling hot oil. Sprinkle with palm sugar and continue frying for a minute or so. Add rice vinegar and return shallots to wok.

Finally, stir in roughly chopped coriander and cook for another few minutes.

Beans in Red Curry Sauce

Wash and clean green beans and halve diagonally if necessary. Wash and shake dry coriander leaves and cut into fine strips.

Heat oil in wok and dissolve curry paste and palm sugar. Add oyster sauce and fish sauce. Then pour in coconut milk and add beans. Leave to cook for about 8 minutes.

Stir in finely chopped coriander, quickly increase heat again and then serve.

Serves 4

1 lb 12 oz/800 g green beans
10 coriander leaves
2 tbsp vegetable oil
2 tbsp red curry paste
1 tbsp palm sugar
4 tbsp oyster sauce
2 tbsp fish sauce
2 cans coconut milk
(1 ⅔ cups/400 ml each)

Preparation time: ca. 20 minutes
Per serving ca. 161 kcal/674 kJ
6 g P, 8 g F, 16 g C

129

Pork Fillet with Soya Sprouts

Serves 4

generous 1 lb/500 g pork fillet

2 tbsp fish sauce

7 oz/200 g shiitake mushrooms

2 carrots

9 oz/250 g soya sprouts

4 tbsp vegetable oil

4 tbsp light soy sauce

a little red chili sauce

a few sprigs Rau Om

Preparation time: ca. 20 minutes (plus marinating time)
Per serving ca. 297 kcal/1246 kJ
32 g P, 14 g F, 12 g C

Wash meat and pat dry. Cut into strips and marinate in fish sauce for 10 minutes.

Clean and slice mushrooms. Clean, wash and peel carrots and cut into slivers. Rinse soya sprouts and shake dry.

Heat oil in wok and quickly sear meat strips. Remove and set aside. Then rapidly sear mushrooms and carrots in wok. Add soya sprouts, return meat to wok, and stir in soy sauce.

Serve in small bowls, drizzle over chili sauce and garnish with Rau Om.

Pork with Garlic

Wash and pat dry meat. Cut into 1 ¼ in/3 cm cubes and marinate in fish sauce for about 10 minutes. Clean, wash and dry beans and cut in half diagonally. Wash and dry chilies and cut into rings. Soak Mu Err mushrooms. Press garlic cloves from bulb and crush without removing skins.

Heat oil and gently sauté garlic cloves. Add beans to garlic and sauté. Then remove and set aside.

Next, rapidly sear meat cubes. Stir in oyster sauce and Nam Prik and then add chilies. Return beans and garlic to wok. Finally, stir in drained mushrooms.

Serves 4

generous 1 lb/500 g pork chop, leg or collar
2 tbsp fish sauce
14 oz/400 g green beans
2 red chilies
3 ½ oz/100 g Mu Err mushrooms
4 tbsp vegetable oil
1 garlic bulb
2 tbsp oyster sauce
1 tsp Nam Prik

Preparation time: ca. 25 minutes
(plus marinating time)
Per serving ca. 427 kcal/1790 kJ
35 g P, 29 g F, 9 g C

Serves 4

generous 1 lb/500 g
sirloin beef

2 tbsp hoisin sauce

1 tbsp honey

½ small cauliflower

7 oz/200 g runner beans

4 tbsp vegetable oil

2 tbsp fish sauce

2 tsp green peppercorns

5 pepper leaves

Preparation time: ca. 15 minutes
(plus marinating time)
Per serving ca. 290 kcal/1214 kJ
29 g P, 15 g F, 8 g C

Marinated Beef Sirloin Strips

Wash and pat dry meat and cut into long thin strips. Marinate in hoisin sauce and honey for 30 minutes.

Clean and wash cauliflower and separate into florets. Clean and wash beans and cut into 2 in/5 cm pieces.

Heat oil in wok. Rapidly sear cauliflower, then remove. Then, repeat the process with beans.

Next, rapidly sear meat strips, return vegetables to wok and drench with fish sauce. Add finely crushed green peppercorns. To finish, stir in chopped pepper leaves.

Beef with Spinach

Wash, dry and cut meat into strips. Rinse spinach well under running water, shake dry and roughly chop. Peel mango and cut into diamond-shaped pieces. Wash and chop chilies.

Heat oil in wok and rapidly sauté spinach with chilies, then remove.

Sear strips of meat in the same oil. Pour in soy sauce and oyster sauce, stirring thoroughly. Then add mango pieces to meat.

Finally, return spinach and chilies to wok and combine with meat. Season with sweet and sour sauce and serve with a scattering of freshly picked Thai basil leaves.

Serves 4

generous 1 lb/500 g beef
7 oz/200 g spinach leaves
1 ripe mango
2 mild green chilies
3 tbsp vegetable oil
2 tbsp soy sauce
2 tbsp oyster sauce
3 tbsp sweet and sour sauce
½ bunch Thai basil

Preparation time: ca. 30 minutes
Per serving ca. 460 kcal/1925 kJ
30 g P, 19 g F, 19 g C

133

Serves 4

generous 1 lb/500 g ground pork
2 eggs
1 bread roll, soaked
salt, pepper
3 tbsp oyster sauce
2 tbsp sweet and sour sauce
3 carrots
7 oz/200 g bamboo shoots
3 ½ oz/100 g spinach
4 tbsp vegetable oil
1 tbsp palm sugar and
1 tbsp red curry paste
3 tbsp fish sauce
2 cans coconut milk
(1 ⅔ cups/400 ml each)

Ground Pork Balls

Preparation time: ca. 35 minutes
Per serving ca. 517 kcal/2167 kJ
34 g P, 33 g F, 19 g C

Combine pork with eggs, bread, salt, pepper, 1 tbsp oyster sauce, and sweet and sour sauce, and form into small walnut-sized mounds.

For the sauce: peel carrots and cut into fine strips with bamboo shoots. Clean, wash and shake dry spinach.

Heat oil in wok, dissolve palm sugar and add curry paste. Drench with fish sauce and 2 tbsp oyster sauce and pour in coconut milk.

Add strips of carrots and bamboo shoots to sauce. Add meatballs and 2 cups/500 ml water and leave to braise for about 10 minutes. At the end, carefully stir in spinach.

Turkey Breast with Chinese Leaves

Wash and pat dry turkey breast, and marinate with spicy bean sauce for 10 minutes.

Wash and peel carrots and cut into slivers. Divide Chinese leaves and remove stalk. Cut leaves into 1 ¼ in/3 cm pieces and wash and shake dry. Wash sugar snaps and cut into diagonal strips. Wash and shake dry coriander and pick off leaves.

Heat half oil in wok, and lightly sauté carrots, cabbage, and sugar snaps. Remove.

Lightly brown curry leaves in remaining oil, add in marinated turkey breast and sauté. Finally, stir in vegetables and coriander leaves.

Serves 4

generous 1 lb/500 g turkey breast
2 tbsp spicy bean sauce
10 ½ oz/300 g carrots
½ Chinese leaves
7 oz/200 g sugar snaps
½ sprig coriander
1 tbsp dried curry leaves
4 tbsp vegetable oil

Preparation time: ca. 20 minutes
(plus marinating time)
Per serving ca. 317 kcal/1326 kJ
35 g P, 12 g F, 13 g C

Steamed Chard Crowns

Serves 4

20 large chard leaves

2 spears lemon grass

1 garlic clove

1 bread roll

⅔ cup/100 g galanga root

generous 1 lb/500 g
ground pork

3 eggs

1 tbsp hoisin sauce

1 tsp finely grated ginger

coriander oil

Preparation time: ca. 50 minutes
Per serving ca. 376 kcal/1576 kJ
34 g P, 20 g F, 11 g C

Wash and quickly blanche chard leaves. Chop 1 spear lemon grass into pieces and finely chop the other with peeled garlic. Soak bread. Peel galanga root and chop into small chunks.

Combine ground pork with eggs, the squeezed, slightly moist bread roll, finely chopped lemon grass and garlic, hoisin sauce and ginger.

Spread filling over blanched chard leaves and form into tiny crowns. Place galangal and lemon grass pieces into bamboo baskets, topping with chard crowns. Drizzle with coriander oil.

Heat water in wok, place bamboo baskets over liquid and steam lidded for about 30 minutes.

Pork Fillet with Limes

Wash and pat dry pork, and dice into ¾ in/2 cm chunks. Marinate for 10 minutes in fish sauce and oyster sauce. Slice limes. Wash and shake dry coriander and pluck off leaves.

Line 4 bamboo baskets with lime pieces, place marinated meat on top and sprinkle with coriander leaves. Cover baskets with lid.

Heat some water in wok and stand baskets over liquid. After 5 minutes, swap top and bottom baskets to ensure even steaming.

Leave covered meat to stand for another 6–8 minutes. Then serve with a sprinkling of red peppercorns.

Serves 4

1 lb 5 oz/600 g pork fillet
4 tbsp fish sauce
4 tbsp oyster sauce
4 limes
1 sprig coriander
4 tsp red peppercorns

Preparation time: ca. 25 minutes
(plus marinating time)
Per serving ca. 205 kcal/858 kJ
35 g P, 6 g F, 6 g C

Chicken Breast in Coconut Milk

Serves 4

4 chicken breasts
10 Kaffir lime leaves
generous 1 ⅓ cups/200 g
cashew nuts
2 tbsp vegetable oil
1 tbsp peanut paste
1 tbsp chili oil
2 cans unsweetened
coconut milk
(1 ⅔ cups/400 ml each)
4 tbsp oyster sauce

Preparation time: ca. 20 minutes
Per serving ca. 617 kcal/2584 kJ
59 g P, 34 g F, 19 g C

Wash and pat dry chicken breasts and cut into strips. Lightly rinse lime leaves and dry. Roughly chop cashews.

Heat oil in wok. Lightly sauté strips of chicken together with peanut paste. Add Kaffir lime leaves, drizzle over chili oil, and continue frying everything.

Pour over coconut milk, stir in oyster sauce and leave to simmer for about 5 minutes. Sprinkle roughly chopped cashew nuts over finished dish.

Beef Curry

Wash and pat dry meat and cut into bite size pieces. Marinate in fish sauce and oyster sauce for 10 minutes. Peel and dice pineapple.

Heat oil in wok, dissolve palm sugar and sweat curry paste. Top up with coconut milk and leave to simmer for about 2 minutes.

Add pineapple pieces, cherry tomatoes, and meat chunks. Continue cooking for about 3 minutes.

Season to taste with a little fish sauce and stir in freshly picked Thai basil leaves. Serve.

Serves 4

generous 1 lb/500 g loin
of beef
2 tbsp fish sauce
3 tbsp oyster sauce
½ pineapple
3 tbsp oil
1 tsp palm sugar and 1 tsp
red curry paste
2 cans unsweetened
coconut milk
(1 ⅔ cups/400 ml each)
7 oz/200 g cherry tomatoes
2 tbsp Thai basil

Preparation time: ca. 20 minutes
(plus marinating time)
Per serving ca. 420 kcal/1759 kJ
31 g P, 16 g F, 39 g C

139

Marinated Lamb

Serves 4

generous 1 lb/500 g leg of lamb

1–2 tbsp tandoori paste

10 ½ oz/300 g cauliflower florets

2 cucumbers

4 tbsp vegetable oil

2 tbsp oyster sauce

3 tbsp fish sauce

2 sprigs coriander

⅔ cup/100 g peanuts

Preparation time: ca. 25 minutes
Per serving ca. 585 kcal/2448 kJ
32 g P, 48 g F, 7 g C

Wash and pat dry lamb, cut into strips and combine with half the tandoori paste. Scrub and wash cauliflower florets. Wash cucumbers, halving them along their length and then dicing diagonally.

Heat half oil in wok. Sear strips of lamb, remove, and set aside.

In remaining oil, rapidly sauté cauliflower and cucumber pieces, and leave to fry until cauliflower is golden yellow. Season with remainder of the tandoori paste and return meat to wok.

Add fish sauce and oyster sauce. Sprinkle with roughly ground peanuts and strips of coriander.

Spicy Chicken

Wash and pat dry chicken breasts. Cut into 1 ¼ in/3 cm cubes. Soak Mu Err mushrooms in water for one hour. Clean spring onions, cut into rings and wash. Wash, dry and de-seed bell peppers, and cut into diamond-shaped pieces. Wash, clean and finely chop chilies.

Heat half oil in wok and sauté bell pepper pieces and spring onions. Remove from wok.

In remaining oil, lightly sear chicken pieces. Return bell peppers and spring onions to wok and stir in chopped chilies. Drench with oyster sauce and fish sauce. Season with chili and garlic sauce.

Drain Mu Err mushrooms and add to wok. Fork through and continue frying for a few minutes. Finally, stir in soya sprouts.

Serves 4

4 chicken breasts
7 oz/200 g dried Mu Err mushrooms
1 bunch spring onions
2 yellow and 2 red bell peppers
2 red chilies
6 tbsp vegetable oil
2 tbsp oyster sauce
4 tbsp fish sauce
1 tsp chili garlic sauce
7 oz/200 g soya sprouts

Preparation time: ca. 30 minutes
Per serving ca. 495 kcal/2073 kJ
68 g P, 21 g F, 11 g C

Beef with Peanut Sauce

Serves 4

generous 1 lb/500 g leg
of beef

2 large onions

4 tbsp vegetable oil

2 tbsp ground peanuts

2 tbsp oyster sauce

1 tbsp palm sugar

1 can unsweetened
coconut milk
(1 ⅔ cups/400 ml)

½ sprig Thai basil

2 tbsp sweet and sour sauce

1 tbsp coarsely chopped
peanuts

Preparation time: ca. 30 minutes
Per serving ca. 410 kcal/1719 kJ
31 g P, 27 g F, 11 g C

Wash, pat dry and cut beef into strips. Peel, halve and slice onions into slivers.

Heat oil in wok. Sauté onions and remove. Sear strips of beef in wok and remove.

Lightly roast chopped peanuts in hot wok. Drench with oyster sauce, sprinkle over palm sugar, pour in coconut milk and allow sauce to thicken.

Return onions and beef to wok and combine well. Finally, season to taste with basil leaves and sweet and sour sauce. Serve sprinkled with roughly chopped peanuts.

Veal with Spicy Coconut Sauce

Wash and pat dry veal fillet and cut into thin ½ in/1 cm strips. Marinate in soy sauce, ginger, and peeled, finely chopped garlic for 10 minutes. Peel baby pineapples and cut into bite size chunks. Quarter and slice lime.

Heat oil in wok. Warm curry paste and blend with coconut milk until smooth. Then stir in remaining coconut milk. Add lime slices and leave to simmer. Season with sugar and fish sauce.

Add pineapple chunks and warm through. Then add meat strips to sauce and leave to braise gently for a few minutes.

Place meat and pineapple in bowls and pour over sauce. Garnish with spots of coconut milk.

Serves 4

1 lb 5 oz/600 g veal fillet
2 tbsp light soy sauce
1 tsp freshly grated ginger
1 garlic clove
2 baby pineapples
1 untreated lime
2 tbsp oil
1 tsp red curry paste
1 can coconut milk
(1 ⅔ cups/400 ml)
pinch of sugar
2 tbsp fish sauce

Preparation time: ca. 20 minutes
(plus marinating time)
Per serving ca. 288 kcal/1204 kJ
34 g P, 8 g F, 16 g C

143

Serves 4

generous 1 cup/150 g unsalted peanuts

1 tbsp each of red curry paste and palm sugar

1 can coconut milk (1 ⅔ cups/400 ml)

7 tbsp water

3 tbsp fish sauce

1 ¼ oz/700 g sea bream

1–2 tbsp tempura flour

6 tbsp sunflower oil

7 oz/200 g broccoli

5 oz/150 g oyster mushrooms

2 flakes green peppercorns, freshly milled

3 tbsp oyster sauce

2 tbsp fish sauce

Preparation time: ca. 40 minutes (plus cooking time)
Per serving ca. 643 kcal/2691 kJ
48 g P, 41 g F, 14 g C

Sea Bream with Peanut Sauce

Dry-roast peanuts in wok until golden brown, allow to cool and grind up finely in a food mixer. Place curry paste, sugar, 7 tbsp coconut milk and water in a saucepan and bring to a boil, stirring continually. Season to taste with fish sauce. Add peanuts and remaining coconut milk, and leave to simmer gently for 15 minutes, stirring occasionally.

Wash and pat dry bream. Starting with the head, slice fish diagonally at ¼ in/½ cm intervals as far as the middle bone. Toss fish slices in tempura flour to coat all over. Place in wok and fry in 3 tbsp oil for about 8 minutes until golden yellow. Then keep warm. Wash broccoli, divide into florets, peel and slice stalk. Clean mushrooms and, depending on size, halve or cut into three slices.

Heat remaining oil in wok. Gradually add broccoli, mushrooms and peppercorn flakes and sear in wok, seasoning with oyster and fish sauce. Arrange fish on top of vegetables and serve with peanut sauce.

Serves 4

4 fillets of sea bream,
unskinned (à 4 ½ oz/
120 g each)
6 medium carrots
4 leeks
4 tbsp vegetable oil
2 tbsp tomato ketchup
4 tbsp sweet and sour sauce
2 tbsp fish sauce
2 sprigs coriander

Preparation time: ca. 25 minutes
Per serving ca. 347 kcal/1455 kJ
31 g P, 16 g F, 15 g C

Sweet and Sour Sea Bream

Wash and pat dry fish fillets and remove bones. Then cut into 1 ¼ in/ 3 cm portions. Wash and peel carrots and slice into strips with peeler. Cut leeks into strips of about 6 in/15 cm, wash and shake dry. Wash and shake dry coriander and pluck off one leaf.

Lightly fry fish portions, skin facing down, in 2 tbsp hot oil in wok. Remove. Sauté vegetables in remaining oil, allow to settle and season with ketchup, sweet and sour sauce, drenching with fish sauce.

Return fish to pot and mix everything carefully together. Finally, stir in the finely chopped coriander. Make sure the sauce doesn't thicken too quickly – you may need to add a little water.

145

Rice with Seafood

Serves 4

1 ¼ cups/250 g long grain rice

4 mild, medium-sized green chilies

4 tbsp vegetable oil

14 oz/400 g mixed ready-prepared seafood

½ cup/100 g fine peas

7 oz/200 g fresh soya sprouts

4 tbsp fish sauce

2 tbsp oyster sauce

1 tsp chili garlic sauce

Preparation time: ca. 30 minutes
Per serving ca. 365 kcal/1530 kJ
23 g P, 14 g F, 35 g C

Cook rice according to instructions on packet and put to one side. Wash and clean chilies and cut into rings.

Heat oil in wok and sear seafood quickly. Add peas and soya sprouts and then stir in cooked rice.

Season to taste with fish sauce, oyster sauce, and chili garlic sauce, and finally stir in chilies.

If the rice starts to stick to the side of the wok, moisten with water.

Serves 4

12 shelled scallops,
without roe

1 knife tip grated,
untreated lemon zest

1 tbsp roasted sesame oil

1 bunch spring onions

7 oz/200 g tomatoes

1 garlic clove

1 red chili

4 tbsp sunflower oil

1 tsp freshly grated ginger

2 tbsp each oyster sauce
and fish sauce

Preparation time: ca. 35 minutes
(plus marinating time)
Per serving ca. 142 kcal/593 kJ
12 g P, 8 g F, 4 g C

Fried Scallops

Wash scallops thoroughly under running water and dry well. Marinate in lemon zest and sesame oil for 10 minutes.

Wash and clean spring onions and cut into 1 ⅔ in/4 cm diagonal strips. Drench tomatoes in boiling water, rinse in cold water, and remove stems and skin. Then cut into quarters, de-seed and slice. Finely chop peeled garlic and de-seeded chili.

Lightly brown spring onions in wok in half oil. Add tomatoes, ginger, garlic, and chili and fry for another 3 minutes. Season with oyster sauce and fish sauce. Remove.

Heat remaining oil in wok and fry scallops until golden yellow. Arrange on dishes with a garnish of spring onions.

Curry with Pike and Water Chestnuts

Serves 4

1 lb 12 oz/800 g fillet of pike

2 tbsp fish sauce

4 ¼ oz/120 g eggplant

1 tbsp red curry paste

1 can coconut milk
(1 ⅔ cups/400 ml)

7 tbsp water

1 tbsp palm sugar

7 oz/200 g water chestnuts

2 Kaffir lime leaves

Preparation time: ca. 30 minutes
(plus marinating time)
Per serving ca. 315 kcal/1320 kJ
47 g P, 3 g F, 25 g C

Wash and pat dry pike fillet and cut into bite size pieces. Marinate in fish sauce for 10 minutes. Wash, dry and dice eggplant.

Combine curry paste in wok with generous ¾ cup/200 ml coconut milk, water and palm sugar and bring to a boil, stirring continuously. Add remaining coconut milk and eggplant and simmer gently for about 10 minutes. Season with fish sauce.

Add well-drained water chestnuts. Add fish pieces and cook for a few minutes.

Cut Kaffir lime leaves into fine strips, mix with fish and serve everything in small bowls.

Lotus Root with Salmon

Wash, pat dry and slice salmon. Wash and brush clean spring onions and cut into fine rings.

Arrange lotus root and salmon in alternating layers. Cover each lotus root with a slice of salmon, coat in fish sauce and drizzle with sesame oil. Continue layering until all ingredients are used up. Finish with a lotus root slice.

Place tartlets into 2 large-sized bamboo baskets. Strew chilies and spring onion rings amongst tartlets.

Place baskets on top of each other in a wok filled with water and steam, lidded, for about 15 minutes. Swap baskets halfway through to ensure even cooking. Serve with a tasty rice vinegar and coriander dip.

Serves 4

14 oz/400 g salmon
1 bunch spring onions
1 can cooked lotus root
(2 ⅔ cups/400 g)
6 tbsp fish sauce
1 tbsp roasted sesame oil
1 handful red chilies
rice vinegar and coriander
leaves for dip

Preparation time: ca. 35 minutes
Per serving ca. 276 kcal/1154 kJ
24 g P, 18 g F, 3 g C

Egg Noodles with Shrimp

Serves 4

9 oz/250 g Chinese egg noodles

10 ½ oz/300 g sugar snaps

1 bunch spring onions

2 small mild green chilies

2 tbsp sesame oil

9 oz/250 g cocktail shrimp

2 tbsp light soy sauce and 2 tbsp sweet and sour chili sauce

6 eggs

salt

Preparation time: ca. 35 minutes
Per serving ca. 562 kcal/2355 kJ
29 g P, 19 g F, 56 g C

Cook egg noodles in salty water according to the instructions on packet. Snip off ends of sugar snaps. Wash, dry and cut them in half diagonally. Wash and clean spring onions and cut into narrow rings. Wash and dry chilies and cut diagonally into fine strips.

Heat sesame oil in wok and sauté spring onions. Stir in first sugar snaps, then chili strips. Add in noodles and continue frying everything for another 3 minutes.

Add shrimp, and season with soy sauce and chili sauce. Push noodle mixture to one side of the wok and pour whisked eggs into the middle. Leave to thicken whilst stirring and then combine with fried noodles.

Salmon with Spinach

Wash and pat dry salmon, then cut into long pieces. Marinate in fish sauce for about 10 minutes. Clean and slice mushrooms. Wash, shake dry and clean spinach.

Heat vegetable and sesame oil in wok, and sauté mushrooms for a short time. Add spinach and let reduce.

Move vegetables over to one side of wok and place salmon pieces in the middle. Sprinkle over sesame seeds and fry carefully. Take care when turning the fish over that it does not fall apart.

Finally, carefully mix vegetables with the fish and season with sambal oelek.

Serves 4

generous 1 lb/500 g
salmon fillet
4 tbsp fish sauce
7 oz/200 g mushrooms
14 oz/400 g fresh spinach
2 tbsp vegetable oil
2 tbsp sesame oil
1 tbsp sesame seeds
1 tsp sambal oelek

Preparation time: ca. 30 minutes
(plus marinating time)
Per serving ca. 480 kcal/2012 kJ
30 g P, 37 g F, 1 g C

Squid with Rice Noodles

Serves 4

9 oz/250 g rice noodles
generous 1 lb/500 g squid
1 bunch coriander
4 tbsp vegetable oil
2 gherkins
2 red dried chilies
4 tbsp oyster sauce
1 tsp sambal oelek

Preparation time: ca. 30 minutes
Per serving ca. 368 kcal/1536 kJ
33 g P, 13 g F, 33 g C

Cook rice noodles according to instructions on the packet and place in a sieve to drain. Clean and wash squid thoroughly. Slit open tubes and fold out with the skin facing downwards. Score with a fine zigzag pattern and then cut into sections. Wash and dry gherkins. Remove seeds and chop into ⅓ in/1 cm pieces. Finely chop coriander leaves in ⅓ in/1 cm strips.

Heat oil in wok. Crush chilies roughly and sear for a short while in oil. Add squid and sear quickly. Then pour over oyster sauce and remove. Put gherkins in wok with 7 tbsp water and allow to steam briefly.

Return squid to wok, and then add cooked rice noodles. Season with sambal oelek and mix in coriander strips. Stir everything to-gether well and serve.

Tuna in Crisp Sesame Jackets

Wash and pat dry tuna fish and cut into 1 ¼ in/3 cm pieces. Combine with fish sauce and toss in sesame seeds.

Wash and dry asparagus and cut into pieces of equal length. Wash and dry horseradish and cut into slivers of about 1 ½ in/4 cm.

Heat 2 tbsp vegetable and sesame oil in wok. Add asparagus and sear briefly. Add horseradish strips and sprinkle with palm sugar. Then remove.

Heat remaining oil and place individual pieces of tuna in wok. Sauté lightly and turn carefully. Finally, return vegetables to wok and pour over oyster sauce. Mix together carefully so everything is evenly covered with sauce and serve immediately.

Serves 4

generous 1 lb/500 g tuna
2 tbsp fish sauce
4 tbsp sesame seeds
1 bundle green asparagus
14 oz/400 g white horseradish
4 tbsp vegetable oil
1 tbsp sesame oil
½ tsp palm sugar
6 tbsp oyster sauce

Preparation time: ca. 25 minutes (plus cooking time)
Per serving ca. 544 kcal/2280 kJ
33 g P, 41 g F, 6 g C

Squid with Broccoli

Serves 4

4 medium squid, fleshy part
1 ¾ lb/800 g broccoli
4 ¼ oz/120 g button
mushrooms
2 garlic cloves
2–3 tbsp sunflower oil
2 tbsp oyster sauce
2 tbsp fish sauce
½ tsp ground coriander
sugar

Preparation time: ca. 25 minutes
Per serving ca. 225 kcal/943 kJ
26 g P, 9 g F, 7 g C

Wash squid thoroughly and pat dry. First, cut open squid on one side, then lay out flat with the inner side pointing upwards. Use a sharp knife to score small ⅟₁₆ in/2 mm diamond shapes on flesh. Then cut squid into 2 in/5 cm sections.

Wash and clean broccoli and break into florets. Peel stem and chop into small pieces. Clean button mushrooms and rub off loose outer layer with kitchen towel. Then cut into quarters. Peel and finely chop garlic.

Pour oil into wok and heat, searing squid for 2 minutes. Remove. Then add garlic, broccoli and mushrooms and lightly brown.

Once this is done, return squid sections to wok and season everything to a spicy taste, adding oyster sauce and fish sauce, coriander and a little sugar.

Serves 4

¾ oz/20 g dried Mu Err
mushrooms
1 medium-sized white
sweetheart cabbage
6 tbsp sunflower oil
1 tbsp oyster sauce
2 tbsp fish sauce
8 scallops, without roe
1 tbsp flour
1 tbsp light soy sauce
2 tbsp hoisin sauce
a little sugar

Preparation time: ca. 30 minutes
(plus soaking time)
Per serving ca. 301 kcal/1258 kJ
20 g P, 15 g F, 19 g C

Scallops with White Cabbage

Soak Mu Err mushrooms for 1 hour in cold water. Halve cabbage, remove stalk and cut each half into fine strips.

Heat 4 tbsp oil in wok, sear about one third of cabbage. Season with oyster sauce, fish sauce, and soy sauce. Repeat this procedure, until remainder of cabbage is used up. Remove and keep warm.

Drain Mu Err mushrooms, clean and chop into small pieces. Halve scallops and sprinkle each half with a dusting of flour, until well coated. Place in wok and fry in rest of hot oil until golden brown, turning so both sides are cooked.

Add Mu Err mushrooms and lightly brown, carefully combining them with cabbage mixture and scallops. To finish, season with soy sauce, hoisin sauce, and sugar.

King Prawns with Oyster Sauce

Serves 4

20 large king prawns,
unpeeled with heads

generous ¾ cup/200 ml
rice wine

6 tbsp vegetable oil

1 tsp palm sugar

4 tbsp oyster sauce

1 tsp chili flakes

Preparation time: ca. 15 minutes
(plus marinating time)
Per serving ca. 305 kcal/1276 kJ
19 g P, 17 g F, 3 g C

Rinse king prawns off thoroughly under tap, dry well and marinate in rice wine for about half an hour.

Pour oil into wok and leave to heat up. Then dissolve palm sugar granules in hot oil and stir in oyster sauce. Add chili flakes and finally king prawns, searing them quickly all over.

Pour marinade over ingredients, cover wok with lid and allow king prawns to cook gently for about 3–5 minutes.

Remove king prawns from wok and arrange on plates. Drizzle with sauce and serve.

Seafood in Ginger Sauce

Simmer 3 quarts/3 l water together with fish sauce and sliced, unpeeled ginger for about 10 minutes and then strain. Wash and shake dry coriander and pluck off the leaves.

Wash, dry and clean zucchini, leek, and carrot. Slice vegetables and cut Kaffir lime in half. Clean and finely slice Shiitake mushrooms.

Wash prawns, scampi, crab and white fish, and pat dry, thoroughly.

Place seafood and vegetables together in wok and pour over ginger stock. Bring mixture to a boil and allow to bubble gently for about 5 minutes. Remove from heat and sprinkle over coriander leaves. To serve, drizzle with chili oil.

Serves 4

6 tbsp fish sauce
2 large pieces ginger
1 bunch coriander
1 zucchini
1 large leek
1 carrot
1 untreated Kaffir lime
3 ½ oz/100 g Shiitake mushrooms
7 oz/200 g prawns
12 scampi
4 swimmer crabs
14 oz/400 g white fish
a little chili oil

Preparation time: ca. 25 minutes
Per serving ca. 310 kcal/1299 kJ
46 g P, 7 g F, 12 g C

Devilfish with Broccoli

Serves 4

4 devilfish fillets, unskinned
2 tbsp fish sauce
2 green chilies
4 spears lemon grass
1 leek
generous 1 lb/500 g broccoli
4 tbsp peanut oil
4 tbsp oyster sauce
1 tbsp grated ginger

Preparation time: ca. 20 minutes
(plus marinating time)
Per serving ca. 388 kcal/1634 kJ
39 g P, 21 g F, 5 g C

Wash and pat dry fish fillets and cut into ¾ in/2 cm wide strips. Marinate in fish sauce as well as small chili rings for about 1 hour.

Cut lemon grass into 2 in/5 cm lengths. Chop leek into rings. Wash broccoli and separate into florets, stripping stalk and cutting it into small chunks.

Heat half peanut oil in wok. Then gently sauté broccoli florets and diced stem pieces, together with lemon grass. Add leek rings and pour in oyster sauce. Finally, stir in grated ginger. Remove everything from wok and keep warm.

Heat remaining peanut oil in wok and add fish pieces. Fry carefully for about 5 minutes over a medium heat, turning so both sides are done. Arrange broccoli and leek on a platter and serve with one fish fillet apiece.

Perch with Red Curry

Wash and pat dry pike fillet and dice into 1 in/3 cm cubes. Marinate in oyster sauce and fish sauce for 30 minutes.

Halve gherkin, removing seeds, and then chop into ⅛ in/½ cm slices. Slice the chili into small rings.

Heat oil in wok and add finely granulated palm sugar and curry paste. Brown lightly, then pour in coconut milk. Bring the mixture to a boil. Add gherkin and leave to simmer gently for 5 minutes.

Drain lychees and add to wok, along with fish pieces. Leave to simmer for about 2 minutes. Finally, toss over chili rings.

Serves 4

generous 1 lb/500 g pike
fillet, skinned
2 tbsp oyster sauce
4 tbsp fish sauce
1 gherkin
1 large dried chili
4 tbsp vegetable oil
1 tbsp palm sugar
1 tbsp red curry paste
2 cans unsweetened
coconut milk
(1 ⅔ cups/400 ml each)
1 can lychees
(à 14 oz/400 g)

Preparation time: ca. 15 minutes
(plus marinating time)
Per serving ca. 318 kcal/1332 kJ
25 g P, 13 g F, 24 g C

159

Index of Recipes